Ruined Cluster

The Spoil

Quinspirus Cluster

Worldsump Ocean

Chem Coasts

Vôsroth

Sulphurous Sea

Sump Coasts

Cog-tooth Bridge

Mortis

Carrion Town

Helmawr's Graveyard

Pie City

Gothrul's Needle

Great Scavic Basin

D1492501

Surverator's Note CY583.7: Not shown on this map is an extensive tunnel network that spans much of the planet. Recent surveys determine that less than 23.9% of this network remains in operative condition.

Hive Primus
The Palatine

9 —

8 — **Imperial House Helmawr**
Lords of the Spire,
Guardians of all Necromunda.

7 —

Great Houses
6 — Greim
Ulanti
Ty
Ran Lo
Catallus
Ko'iron

5 —

4 — Hab Zones
Manufactory Zones
Ruined Manufactories

Clan Houses
3 — Cawdor
Escher
Goliath
Van Saar
Orlock
Delaque

2 —

1 —

External
Shanty Sprawl

Lower Atmospheric Level

Imperial Fists
Chapter House

The Shell

Landing Field

The Spire

The Wall

Cloud Cover

Subsidary Spires

Hive City

Poisonous Undercloud

The Stranger's Spire

Current Surface Level

The Underhive

Hive Bottom

The Sump

Primary Heat Sink

Surverator's rendering, commissioned for Lady Jin Ulanti, M41.112971.

NECROMUNDA

On Necromunda, truth spills from the mouth of Lord Helmawr, and all other voices only whisper lies, rumours and falsehoods, fleeting as the passing of cycles.

A cog in a machine need not know its purpose to function, only that it must turn and bite its fellows with its teeth, so speaks the voice of the Imperial House. Look down upon your tasks, never raise your gaze to the spire lest it blind you with its light. You are needed, you are vital, your toils are key to the wellbeing of your world and the walls that keep the horrors of the wastes at bay. You are disposable, you are meaningless, your efforts are as the death rattle of the dying – pointless and wasted. Embrace the lie that gives you purpose and cast off the truth that screams you are a captive ape rotting on a dead world in an ancient cage of plasteel and ferrocrete.

Gangs are those who reject these lies, the dispossessed who rage against their fate and strain against their fetters, unaware that they too keep the wheel turning with their disobedience.

CONTENTS

2

Games Workshop Web site: www.games-workshop.com
Forge World Web site: www.forgeworld.co.uk

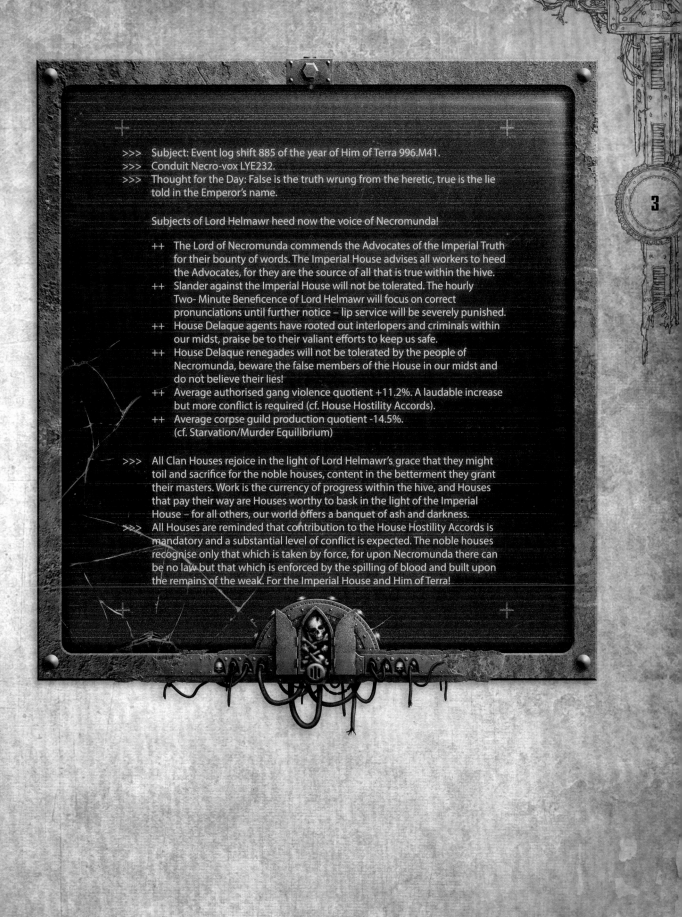

>>> Subject: Event log shift 885 of the year of Him of Terra 996.M41.
>>> Conduit Necro-vox LYE232.
>>> Thought for the Day: False is the truth wrung from the heretic, true is the lie told in the Emperor's name.

Subjects of Lord Helmawr heed now the voice of Necromunda!

++ The Lord of Necromunda commends the Advocates of the Imperial Truth for their bounty of words. The Imperial House advises all workers to heed the Advocates, for they are the source of all that is true within the hive.
++ Slander against the Imperial House will not be tolerated. The hourly Two-Minute Beneficence of Lord Helmawr will focus on correct pronunciations until further notice – lip service will be severely punished.
++ House Delaque agents have rooted out interlopers and criminals within our midst, praise be to their valiant efforts to keep us safe.
++ House Delaque renegades will not be tolerated by the people of Necromunda, beware the false members of the House in our midst and do not believe their lies!
++ Average authorised gang violence quotient +11.2%. A laudable increase but more conflict is required (cf. House Hostility Accords).
++ Average corpse guild production quotient -14.5%. (cf. Starvation/Murder Equilibrium)

>>> All Clan Houses rejoice in the light of Lord Helmawr's grace that they might toil and sacrifice for the noble houses, content in the betterment they grant their masters. Work is the currency of progress within the hive, and Houses that pay their way are Houses worthy to bask in the light of the Imperial House – for all others, our world offers a banquet of ash and darkness.
>>> All Houses are reminded that contribution to the House Hostility Accords is mandatory and a substantial level of conflict is expected. The noble houses recognise only that which is taken by force, for upon Necromunda there can be no law but that which is enforced by the spilling of blood and built upon the remains of the weak. For the Imperial House and Him of Terra!

WARS OF THE UNDERHIVE

The underhive lies beneath the hive cities, beyond the laws of House and hive. Its depth varies from a few hundred metres to several kilometres, and its extent is neither constant nor strictly delineated, the crumbling margins of the hive above simply melting into the upper zones of the underhive. It is a no-man's land: the Badzones… downhive. Here an individual can make a new beginning or come to a sudden end, and everyone knows there are fortunes to be won in the depths for those willing to take the chance.

The physical structure of the underhive is the same as the rest of the hive. It is speculated that most hives began as a single hab dome of plascrete or some other highly durable material. Over the years, more domes were added together with tunnels and shafts to connect them. Eventually, new domes were built on top of the old, and further domes were raised on top of these, producing a honeycomb of large enclosed spaces. The thick outer walls were added later to protect the towering structure and it is the foundations of these man-made caverns that give the hives their structural integrity.

Like the manufactory zones far above, the interior spaces of the underhive often take the form of unimaginably vast, industrial-scaled cathedrals of ferrous-decay. Long abandoned and sometimes fallen unto rust, the ancient machines of these zones are far beyond functioning and often merge into the structure of the hive itself. Mechanisms the size of battleships slowly rust into mountains of slag, their original function long forgotten. Some may bear a spark of machine life yet however, occasionally powering up into spontaneous un-life to crush the unwary in cyclopean pistons. It is said that gangs of particularly debased underhive mutants worship these machines as hungry gods, sacrificing captives upon their iron altars.

A dome provides a broad open space which is further divided into zones of factories, houses, commercial buildings and myriad other structures. Each dome sits upon a deep foundation layer which incorporates a sub-level maze of power lines and supply pipes. Larger domes also have tall reinforcing pillars which support the roof. The geography of the hive is therefore one of a series of interconnected domes or caverns linked by major tunnelways or shafts, and divided internally into built-up areas.

Between each dome is to be found a labyrinth of tunnels, some used as accessways to vital hive infrastructure, others decayed and long forgotten. It is amongst this maze that the most bitter of wars are often fought, far from the gaze of the enforcers, the gangs using them to infiltrate far into enemy territory in order to launch daring and bloody raids.

SELENE VEGA
HELL'S OWN
HOUSE ESCHER

BATTLES IN THE BADZONES

It is with good reason that hivers often refer to the underhives of Necromunda as the Badzones. The hab and manufactory areas of the hives are dark, polluted and decaying, but the underhive is a hundred times worse. Its domed caverns are dark and ruinous. Collapsed floors and fallen buildings have reduced many areas to waste zones of rubble and debris, and poisonous effluvia, toxic dust and the filth of the hive seep downwards and bury everything in a thick layer of detritus.

The underhive has a geography all of its own and fighting through it is a battle in itself, regardless of the intentions of a gang's rivals. Amongst the tangle of ruins there are isolated pockets which can be made habitable with a little effort and these are therefore worth fighting over. In places the rubble conceals remnants of previous occupation – machinery or artefacts which can be reclaimed or traded, and these are fought over especially hard by gangs. Scattered across the underhive are outcrops of naturally formed ores or ancient refuse which can yield rare and valuable minerals. Entire regions remain unexplored, and much of the hive is unreachable because of blocked and flooded tunnels. Plenty of domes are simply waste zones, neither habitable nor containing anything of obvious worth.

Tunnels and vertical shafts link the domed chambers together and these are the sites of constant battles to control passage. The tunnel structures are weaker than the domes they serve, so they are often destroyed or partially blocked even if the dome itself is intact. Sometimes a narrow crawl hole in the debris may allow a person to squeeze through, but these tunnels are dangerous and often lead nowhere or end in flooded sumps or sudden drops. The entire underhive is thus a complex maze where it is only too easy to become disorientated and lost, and gangs will pay richly for the services of a scout able to guide them into the heart of a rival group's territory using such hidden ways.

Many hundreds of metres below ground level, the depths of the underhive give way to the collapsed and compacted ruins of the hive bottom, the ancient foundation layer long since abandoned and forgotten by its inhabitants. This is a domain of stagnant darkness, where poisoned fumes rise from the putrid sump lake at the hive's bottom and choke the labyrinth of crude crawl holes and ruinous caverns. Here in the darkness dwell things spawned in the toxic waste of millennia, creatures that hide from even the pallid lights of the underhive. Sometimes they crawl from their holes, slithering up from the blackness, driven by their hunger, perhaps, for human flesh and blood. Their eyes can be seen glimmering amongst the ruins as they study the progress of a slave train, watching for stragglers and the wounded.

Throughout the underhive they can be heard howling and snarling in the dark hours of lights-out, always close by yet always unseen, a sound to haunt the sleep. Occasionally, a hunter or an ore prospector might bring in a pelt of some strange bestial thing. Some of them are men, or once were, with scabrous rotting skin and talon-like nails, eyes vestigial and covered with white membranes, or black and staring without visible iris. Others have only the sham of human form, scaly and vile things with dripping maws of pointed teeth and long red tongues. Over the far wall of the Down Town trade hole, there are nailed the skins of many such beasts, hundreds upon hundreds of them, some rotten and eaten away by time or infestation, others gleaming with green and golden scales, a few of the skins of savages and outlaws brought in for bounty.

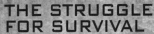

THE STRUGGLE FOR SURVIVAL

Despite the appalling conditions, there is no shortage of people seeking to make their home in the underhive. The discontented, the poor, the disinherited and outcasts naturally gravitate downhive, away from the power of the Guild and family patriarchs, and these refugees from uphive are sometimes called 'green hivers' by established downsiders.

The Badzones are a place of opportunity for impoverished hivers who are unable or unwilling to endure hive life. With hard work, tunnels can be opened up, generators and air pumps can be installed, effluent flows can be diverted and water stills erected. Slurry pits and hive dust can be coaxed to yield crops of algae, mutant fungus and nutritious slime. Over the years order can be restored and eventually an area may even be reclaimed and re-integrated into the hive itself.

Underhive communities tend to be small affairs, a few simple holes and dens rather than entire towns. There are also some fair sized and well-established settlements such as Dust Falls and Dead End Pass far beneath Hive Primus. Larger downhive settlements are often protected by tall stockades which the inhabitants raise out of the surrounding debris. Shelters and other buildings are converted from the ruins, and materials scavenged from the refuse. It is possible to survive by cultivating edible fungi, algae, slime or the parasitic lichen that grows upon them, and in some places, settlers raise animals native to the Badzones such as rats, blood beetles, giant slugs, blind snakes and mutant dogs.

The bigger settlements have a kind of order, albeit utterly unlike the strict social codes of the hive cities themselves. There are places to trade, small workshops where equipment can be made or repaired, and people offering services to travellers. A bed for the night, a room, an annual bath, or just food and drink, all can be readily bought or bartered. The most valuable commodity of all though is often information. News of ore strikes and tunnel openings are typical of the rumours that can make a man rich if he's quick enough!

TRADE WARS

Most settlements have trade posts where Guilders sell their wares or buy things that have been found, made or stolen in the underhive, and sometimes they hire gang fighters to protect themselves or their cargoes. The Guilders' heavily guarded slave trains carry goods within the underhive, and between the underhive and the hive city above. In larger communities it is the Guilders that really run things. Anyone trying to cheat or harm a Guilder soon meets with rough justice as Guilders are notoriously protective of their own kind, and will hunt down anyone who kills or robs from them. Nonetheless, Guilders are not immune from attack and their cargoes are a favourite target for outlaw gangs. Poorer Guilders sometimes strike out alone, chasing rumours of ore strikes or finds of archaeotech. For every lone explorer that makes their way back to a settlement like Dust Falls, likely as not mad-eyed with their clothes in tatters and babbling of untold riches, a hundred are never seen again. The underhive simply swallows them up.

ORES AND MINERALS

Some hivers come to the Badzones to make their fortune from the vast natural wealth of the underhive. Pollutants transmute over the millennia, gradually losing their toxic properties and forming new stable compounds, including sparstone, adonite crystals, carnotite gems and dark nuggets of igneous adamantorite. These precious substances are found in the deeper parts of the underhive at the hive bottom. Rich deposits are very rare and searching for them amongst the poisonous wastes is hazardous. Mineral ore deposits are more common and these often originate from liquid discharges from the hive above. Working their way downwards, ore-laden wastes reach open spaces and form stalagmites and stalactites of ferrous haematite or 'iron slag'. Some pollutant liquids filter through porous wastes which act as sieves, depositing solid ore in the form of a crust or pan. These substances are bulky and not tremendously valuable, but their exploitation is relatively easy.

Ore diggers work either on their own or in groups. They often build temporary shelters round the site of a strike, and may well have to defend their workings from marauding outlaw gangs. The richer the find, the more attention it draws from jealous eyes, such that years of bitter gang warfare might be fought in order to protect an ore site from its owner's rivals, drawing in mercenary gangs and hired guns from all around the region.

HIVE FUNGUS

Great wealth can be gleaned from the mutant fungoid life forms which grow in the dark underhive. The detritus of the downhive provides the ideal medium for fungi to grow in and, as a result, the underhive supports a substantial ecology of parasites and mutant creatures. There are tens of thousands of varieties of fungi and moulds, some of them are edible or otherwise useful, others highly toxic and downright dangerous.

Rare fungi are much sought after. The slow growing pearl spore forms tiny lustrous pearls within its flesh; the colour and quality of individual 'pearls' depending upon which pollutants the fungus grows upon as well as its age. The most valuable of all is the Necromundan black pearl, a single large example of which is sufficient to keep a person in life-long luxury. Iron mould is not valuable in itself, but grows on rust piles and detritus saturated with sequestered iron and other metals. The mould extracts water and bound oxygen from the substrate, leaving nodules of metal underneath.

Other fungi have medical or intoxicant properties. Examples include the dangerous and costly icrotic slime. The possession of living icrotic slime is one of the most serious crimes in many hive cities and its export from Necromunda is forbidden by Imperial decree. Ghast is the most notorious fungal form, a psychic stimulant formed from fungal spoor growing on ancient caches of corpse-starch. More useful is the curative stinger mould, which has powerful recuperative abilities as well as strong antibiotic properties.

THE HUNT FOR ARCHAEOTECH

Much of the underhive is unexplored or inaccessible and amongst the ruins lie factories, machines, stockpiles of raw materials and stores of artefacts buried millennia ago. Sudden structural catastrophes are not uncommon in the lower parts of the hive, so it is easy to imagine how a collapsed dome could be buried along with its inhabitants. Over time the dome will be forgotten, waste leaks in from above, and layers of hive dust pile on top of the ruins. All this can remain untouched for centuries, perhaps for millennia, until erosion or a hive quake opens up a small crawl hole into the ancient dome. When a tunnel into a new area is discovered, it becomes a magnet for fortune hunters, as well as those who would forcibly take what others have earned. Any attempt at secrecy can only succeed for a short while, and soon the dome will be teeming with rivals. Inevitably, there will be battles over the spoils, and the victors will carry away the choicest items for themselves.

Archaeotech is the term given to ancient technological artefacts. The richest source of archaeotech is lost domes, but it is possible to find old machines or components at the bottom of any deep layer of hive debris. The value of an item depends very much on what it is. Old rusted machinery is only good for scrap and will have to be sold for the value of the metal it contains. Isotropic crystal fuel rods, on the other hand, remain viable so long as they are unused, and can be traded for a good price.

FLOTSAM AND JETSAM

The underhive exists beyond the laws of House and hive. The Great Houses have little influence and clan patriarchs care little about life beyond their borders. Even the Imperial House would think twice about trying to impose its will in the anarchic bowels of the hive. The underhive provides a natural refuge for those seeking to escape retribution or revenge, for criminals and dissidents can melt into society without fear. Larger groups of outcasts can find a secluded place to make their home, amongst them crazed religious zealots, mutant-hating Redemptionists, Utopionists, cannibals, head-hunters and any number of misfits and madmen.

Amongst those who have taken refuge in the underhive are members of the ruling line itself. When Lord Marius Helmawr was murdered centuries ago, his surviving son, Caetrus, fled into the depths beneath Hive Primus where he became a celebrated outlaw leader and popular hero. Although his uncle Lord Tiberius Helmawr tried to capture or kill Caetrus for many years, he never succeeded. The Delaque agents sent to root out Caetrus and his followers were finally forced to admit defeat and Caetrus lived to reclaim his birthright after Tiberius' death, but never forgot his underhive years and rewarded his supporters generously. Though Tiberius is long dead, rumour persists of lost branches of the Helmawr bloodline living in the underhive, biding their time until they unite the masses, rise up and reclaim their birthright.

ULZCHA THE KNIFE
SILKEN GLOOM
HOUSE DELAQUE

RATSKIN RAIDS

The Ratskin people are said to have lived in the ruins of the underhive for as long as time itself, and they regard the place as their ancestral home. They know almost nothing about the world that lies above their heads or beyond the hive shell, and have lived apart for so long that they have developed their own language, and only the few of their kind who visit the underhive settlements to trade bother to learn the common tongue of the hive.

Ratskins possess senses uniquely adapted to the conditions of the underhive. Their sight is incredibly keen and it is commonly supposed they can see in pitch darkness. A Ratskin can smell out tiny differences in air quality and can track other hivers or hive creatures by scent. Their hearing is also finely attuned to the hive and the slightest sounds tell them where others might be, whether a tunnel is safe, or if dangerous creatures lurk nearby.

Ratskins care nothing for the spires or the hivers that come from above. They do not understand the hivers' insane lust for scrap metals and glittering stones. Most of all they are baffled by the foolish manner in which settlers eat toxic fungus, fall down holes, blunder into roof falls, and generally act in a senseless and dangerous fashion. Although the outsiders puzzle and often anger them, they are content to leave hivers alone so long as they leave the Ratskins in peace. Adventurous Ratskins will trade with the hivers and sometimes hire themselves out as guides or trackers, but they are generally a self-sufficient and proud people who neither need nor want much from the outsiders.

Ratskins know their way around the underhive better than anyone else. They know about the main tunnels, the small crawl holes, and the shifting drains and sumps of the effluvial flows. They know ways into and through the underhive, ways which the hivers are utterly ignorant of, and can find paths into domes which remain undiscovered and buried to ordinary people. Ratskins move through the hives effortlessly and mysteriously, disappearing almost magically and then reappearing as if from nowhere.

Some Ratskins hire themselves out as guides or trackers, and a few become semi-civilised as a result of contact with hivers and can be found and hired in the larger settlements such as Dead End Pass of Hive Primus. There are few expeditions that would venture into unknown waste zones without the expert aid of a Ratskin tracker. Sadly, some Ratskins are attracted to the strange ways of the hivers, and acquire a taste for intoxicants, gambling and riotous living. These troublesome individuals hang around the settlements until their inhabitants lose patience and throw them out into the wastes. When these outcasts do occasionally form into bands of Ratskin renegades, they are a nuisance to settlers and their own kin, and have a well-deserved reputation for savagery.

GANGS OF THE UNDERHIVE

This book represents the culmination of a lot of hard work. It has only been a year since the release of Necromunda: Underhive, and in that time, the game has grown immeasurably. With five of the noble houses already represented on the battlefields of the underhive, and the sixth debuting here, players now have the ability to represent the House of their choosing. Each gang has been expanded with the addition of Hangers-on, Exotic Beasts and mighty Brutes, not to mention Hired Guns in the form of Bounty Hunters and Underhive Scum. The game itself has grown beyond recognition as well, with the addition of many new scenarios, Arbitrator tools, and a vastly expanded set of rules for playing stand-alone Skirmish games that easily enable organised events to take place, be they competitive or narrative. Alongside a whole new campaign system, players have tremendous choice in how they explore the darkness of the underhive.

Gangs have enjoyed gaining access to a huge array of equipment through the ever-growing Trading Post, along with the introduction of many new types of weaponry, Wargear and a host of new special rules and Weapon Traits. Be it fluttering servo-skulls or access to Exotic Goods, up-and-coming gang leaders can now show their power with ostentatious displays of wealth.

But more than that, the past year has seen hobbyists the world over playing an uncountable number of games. This has generated a huge amount of feedback and some very good questions. In attempting to answer these, and by paying careful heed to this invaluable feedback, this book has evolved.

Gangs of the Underhive contains updated rosters for Houses Cawdor, Escher, Goliath, Orlock and Van Saar. Debuting here is the all-new House Delaque gang roster, extensively playtested alongside these other rosters. Beside this are updated rules for Hired Guns, Hangers-on, Brutes and Exotic Beasts, as well as an even larger Trading Post and the most complete equipment reference section to date. Combined with updated Weapon Traits, skills and Wargear rules, and many adjusted credits values, *Gangs of the Underhive* contains everything a player could need to found their own gang and take to the underhive.

At every opportunity, the rules contained within this book have been edited and clarified in order to maintain balance and ease of use, all of it informed by the valuable feedback we have received from you, the players. The rules here will work equally as well with the *Necromunda: Underhive* rulebook, as they will with the all-new, fully updated *Necromunda Rulebook* released alongside, the intent of which is to give an even richer gaming experience for Necromunda players.

HOUSE GANGS

When founding a Necromunda gang, the first step is to decide which House the gang is drawn from. The rules which follow cover the six Clan Houses of Necromunda: Cawdor, Delaque, Escher, Goliath, Orlock and Van Saar.

When founding a gang, players will have a maximum budget of credits to spend. How much this is will depend upon whether they are founding a gang for Skirmish or Campaign play. In either case, this budget may not be exceeded. Any unspent credits will be added to the gang's Stash if the gang has been founded for Campaign play. However, if a gang has been founded for Skirmish play, any unspent credits are simply lost.

The next step is to choose the fighters that make up the gang. The following House lists show the fighters available to each gang. A fighter's entry in their House list will detail the weapon types they may be armed with, as well as listing any Wargear they have when added to the gang. Whenever a fighter is added to a gang, weapons and Wargear are purchased for them. If the gang is being founded for a campaign, fighters will be limited to equipment selected from their House Equipment List, whereas fighters in a gang founded for a Skirmish may also have access to some items of equipment from the Trading Post. In either case, a fighter may discard any Wargear they have in favour of something else purchased from the House Equipment list (most commonly this will be armour). Wargear discarded when a gang is founded is placed in the gang's Stash and may be given to other fighters.

Finally, a blank Fighter card is completed for each fighter when they are added to the gang; the characteristics of the fighter and any equipment they now have should be noted down in the appropriate sections of the Fighter card. A gang roster sheet is also completed for the gang as a whole, following the guidelines given for campaign play (see page 81) or skirmish play (see page 109) within the *Necromunda Rulebook*.

GANG COMPOSITION

All gangs follow these rules when they are founded:
- There must be one Leader.
- The total number of Gangers in the gang must always be equal to, or higher than, the total number of other fighters (Leaders, Juves and Champions) in the gang, not counting Hangers-on.
- A fighter can be equipped with a maximum of three weapons. Weapons marked with an asterisk (*) take up the space of two weapons.
- Any fighter may take Wargear.
- Weapon accessories marked with a dagger (†) may not be combined together on the same weapon. If one such accessory is purchased for a weapon, another may not be added.

During a campaign, all gangs continue to follow the above rules as new fighters are added to the gang. Additionally, the following rules apply:
- A gang founded for a campaign can contain no more than two Champions. Additional Champions may be added to the gang during the course of the campaign.
- During the course of a campaign, any fresh recruits added to the gang may be equipped with items currently held in the gang's Stash, rather than purchasing new equipment.
- During the course of the campaign, gangs may gain new equipment, either by purchasing it from the Trading Post or as a result of Territory Boons. These items are added to the gang's Stash and may be distributed among fighters during any Post-battle sequence:
  - A fighter cannot be given a new weapon of a type not allowed by their entry within their House list.
  - Juves and Gangers cannot be given a new weapon if it would take them above the limit of three weapons carried.
  - A Leader or Champion can be given more than three weapons as they can have multiple Fighter cards, each representing a different 'set' of equipment, as described on page 95 of the *Necromunda Rulebook*.
  - A fighter may discard any Wargear carried when given new Wargear. Discarded Wargear is placed in the gang's Stash.

COTTLE SCRUTTOR
THE HANGED
HOUSE CAWDOR

GANGS OF HOUSE CAWDOR

The men and women of House Cawdor are the bonepickers, scrap herders and midden-thieves of Necromunda, their vast empire built upon the discarded scraps of the other clans and bound together by an unshakeable faith. The House owes much of its existence to the Cult of the Redemption – a splinter sect of the Imperial Cult that emerged on Necromunda centuries ago, its preachers proclaiming the doom of the Imperium and the unworthiness of Mankind to all who would listen. Of all of the Houses to entertain the Redemption's demagogues, only the rubbish-peddlers of Cawdor took their message so utterly to heart – embracing their own inferiority and pledging their worthless lives to the spreading of the faith. Though faith has done little for the House's wealth, its people have endured where other Houses have failed and fallen to the march of time. Now the clan is equal in size, though not in wealth or status, to several of the other Clan Houses combined – not least of all because Cawdor has a long history of gathering up outcasts and, many claim, kidnapping the children of other clans.

Devotion to the Cult of the Redemption guides the actions of all members of House Cawdor. From their first days in the orphanarium-fanes, the snatchlings of the House are taught that the doom of the universe hangs eternal over their heads. Only by giving themselves utterly to the Emperor can their otherwise worthless lives have meaning, and only by serving the clan's word-keepers will the Master of Mankind hear their faint prayers. Cawdor men and women live segregated lives, ruled over by the Emperor's word and existing in a state of poverty extreme even by the standards of Necromunda. Its people make their meagre wealth by scavenging through the refuse of the hive, unearthing 'blessed' relics from amongst the rubbish. The Cult teaches that material belongings are fleeting, as is the importance of the individual – thus do Cawdor workers keep only those possessions deemed to be of spiritual significance, while they hide their faces behind masks so that the Emperor might not think them too proud of their individuality.

Given the poverty that grips House Cawdor, most of the House's allied gangs favour simple and effective weaponry; the battered autogun, the trusty stub gun and the rusty knife are all good enough for a Cawdor ganger. In fact, Cawdor gangs have a special talent for restoring discarded guns and blades, scraping together a working weapon from the parts of several others or making a new weapon onto which they can painstakingly carve the scriptures of their faith. Fire is a favoured tool of the gangs, for it is simple to use and, like the doom that devours the galaxy, consumes all in its path. Creating incendiary grenades, flamers and other fire-based weapons is a simple task within a hive, for the flammable fuel and waste lines that run through the great city's walls are easily syphoned off. In combat, killing a foe in the white-hot furnace of a well-placed flamer burst, or in the blinding halo of a fire bomb, is an almost holy act for a Cawdor ganger,

the piteous screams of the heretic as they burn a benediction to the Emperor, proclaiming for all to hear the true majesty of the Redemption.

The ideals of the Cult of the Redemption thrive in places where the word of the Imperial Creed is but a distant, half-heard echo. Cawdor gangs are usually tasked to bring the word of the Cult to the shadowy depths of the underhive, the wilderness between the hives or the abandoned ruins of places left behind by the relentless march of millennia. Here, many despair that the Emperor and the Imperium have forsaken them, and so are easy converts to the portents of doom and darkness offered up by the Redemption. Each gang then becomes a church unto itself, servicing a flock of followers, and when they fight back against the interests of other clans or the indifference of the hive lords, they further cement their position as saviours. Most gangs are ruled by a powerful patriarch, with women forbidden to take up arms for the House. And yet, just as the men of Cawdor are driven by their faith, so too are there all-women Cawdor gangs. These have their own word-keepers and traditions that teach that all in His eyes are warriors for the cause. Some of these female gangs are formed as distorted reflections of the militant orders of the Adepta Sororitas – with names like the Ash Rose Covenant or the Sisters of the Ragged Shroud, and they can be even more ferocious than their male counterparts.

The history of House Cawdor is littered with the tales of scrap-saints and ash-martyrs. Among these stories the most common is that of Caul the Fallen, the first pilgrim of the Red Redemption. So it goes, Caul left the shelter of his hive in search of relics in the wilds of Necromunda. Across the wastelands he wandered, and where he went cults sprung up from the dust in his wake. He won countless battles against heretics, monsters and mutants alike, his righteous soldiers vanquishing the Ember Lords of the Yearning Deeps, and murdering the Dark Arbitrators that once ruled the lost hives of Spoilshadow to a man. Even now,

centuries later, Caul's masked visage stares down from tumbled spires and broken wrecks, a reminder that the glory of the Redemption lives eternal.

Then there are the gangs that have found their own faith among the splinters of the Redemption. Hauberk Halfhand is the pitiless master of the Broken Ones. After having his spine shattered by an Orlock bullet and lying dying for days in the stygian depths of Hive Primus, Hauberk gazed into the abyss of hive bottom and the abyss gazed back at him. In the depths of his despair, Hauberk came to see that only the truly broken can fully understand the faith, and so, once he had crawled back to a settlement, he drew to himself the mangled cast-offs from other Cawdor gangs – he himself stitched back together to be born anew. The Broken Ones are now a scourge upon Hive Primus, destroying everything in their path so it might be welcomed into the faith. Their foes are all given the same choice; to have their bones and bodies smashed by Hauberk so they might join his gang – or if they reject the faith, the finality of the void.

Perhaps the greatest living warrior of the Redemption is the Thane of Cawdor, Lord Mormaer. Legend has it that he rose up from among the bonepickers of Hive Primus, making a name for himself in the depths of the underhive by building blazing heretic pyres and unearthing ancient Ministorum relics. When the old Thane was close to death, he sought out Mormaer as his replacement, for, as the story goes, it is each Thane's right to choose a successor from among the most faithful of their servants. It is this promise of faith rewarded with rulership that drives many Cawdor gang leaders. However, proving worthy of ascension is an elusive task, if it is even possible at all – there being just as many that believe the whole tale is one created by Mormaer himself to keep the faithful true.

BARBET 'THE BRUTE'
THE HANGED
HOUSE CAWDOR

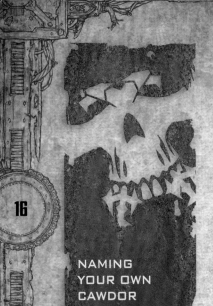

FIGHTERS

A starting Cawdor gang is made up of the following fighters:

LEADER .... 105 CREDITS

M	WS	BS	S	T	W	I	A	Ld	Cl	Wil	Int
5"	3+	4+	3	3	2	4+	2	4+	6+	5+	6+

EQUIPMENT

A Cawdor Leader is equipped with flak armour. They have no weapon restrictions.

STARTING SKILL

Cawdor Leaders start with one free skill chosen from their Primary skill sets.

CHAMPIONS .... 95 CREDITS EACH

M	WS	BS	S	T	W	I	A	Ld	Cl	Wil	Int
5"	4+	3+	3	3	2	4+	2	5+	6+	7+	6+

EQUIPMENT

A Cawdor Champion is equipped with flak armour. They have no weapon restrictions.

STARTING SKILL

Cawdor Champions start with one free skill chosen from their Primary skill sets.

JUVES .... 20 CREDITS EACH

M	WS	BS	S	T	W	I	A	Ld	Cl	Wil	Int
6"	5+	5+	3	3	1	3+	1	8+	8+	8+	9+

EQUIPMENT

A Cawdor Juve starts with no equipment. They can be armed with Pistols and Close Combat Weapons, but cannot be given any item that is worth more than 20 credits when they are added to the gang. During a campaign, once a Juve has gained their first Advancement, this limit no longer applies.

GANGERS .... 45 CREDITS EACH

M	WS	BS	S	T	W	I	A	Ld	Cl	Wil	Int
5"	4+	4+	3	3	1	4+	1	7+	7+	7+	7+

EQUIPMENT

A Cawdor Ganger is equipped with flak armour. They can be armed with Basic Weapons, Close Combat Weapons and Pistols. When the gang is created, one Ganger can be armed with a Special Weapon. During a campaign, additional Gangers can also take Special Weapons as they are added.

SKILL ACCESS

Cawdor fighters have access to the following skills.

	Agility	Brawn	Combat	Cunning	Ferocity	Leadership	Shooting	Savant
Leader	-	Primary	Primary	-	Secondary	Primary	-	Secondary
Champion	Secondary	Primary	Primary	-	Secondary	Secondary	-	-
Juve	Secondary	-	Secondary	-	Primary	-	-	-
Specialist	Secondary	Secondary	Primary	-	Primary	-	-	-

HOUSE CAWDOR EQUIPMENT LIST

WEAPONS

BASIC WEAPONS
- Cawdor polearm/autogun*...................... 20 credits
- Cawdor polearm/blunderbuss*
  (with grape & purgation shot)................ 40 credits
- Reclaimed autogun.............................. 10 credits
- Sawn-off shotgun................................ 15 credits

CLOSE COMBAT WEAPONS
- Axe... 10 credits
- Chain glaive*.................................... 60 credits
- Maul (club)...................................... 10 credits
- Fighting knife .... 15 credits
- Flail.. 20 credits
- Two-handed axe* .... 25 credits
- Two-handed hammer* .... 35 credits

PISTOLS
- Hand flamer .... 75 credits
- Reclaimed autopistol........................... 5 credits
- Stub gun .... 5 credits

SPECIAL WEAPONS
- Combi weapon (autogun/flamer)........... 110 credits
- Flamer .... 130 credits
- Long rifle .... 30 credits

HEAVY WEAPONS
- Cawdor heavy crossbow*
  (with frag & krak shells) .... 125 credits
- Heavy flamer* .... 195 credits
- Heavy stubber*................................. 130 credits

WARGEAR

GRENADES
- Blasting charges.............................. 35 credits
- Choke gas grenades .... 50 credits
- Frag grenades................................. 30 credits
- Incendiary charges........................... 40 credits
- Krak grenades .... 45 credits
- Smoke grenades............................... 15 credits

ARMOUR
- Flak armour .... 10 credits
- Mesh armour .... 15 credits

PERSONAL EQUIPMENT
- Bomb delivery rats .... 30 credits
- Cult icon.. 40 credits
- Drop rig... 10 credits
- Dumdum rounds (for stub gun) .... 5 credits
- Emperor's Wrath rounds (for blunderbuss) 35 credits
- Filter plugs.................................... 10 credits
- Mono-sight† .... 35 credits
- Photo-goggles .... 35 credits
- Respirator .... 15 credits
- Skinblade....................................... 10 credits
- Strip kit.. 15 credits

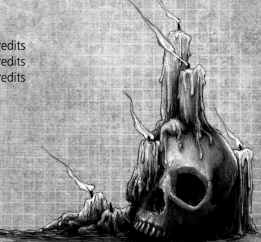

HOUSE CAWDOR WEAPONRY

TWO-HANDED HAMMER

MAUL (CLUB)

FIGHTING KNIFE

RECLAIMED AUTOPISTOL

RECLAIMED AUTOPISTOL

RECLAIMED AUTOPISTOL

MAUL (CLUB)

STUB GUN

FLAIL

FLAMER

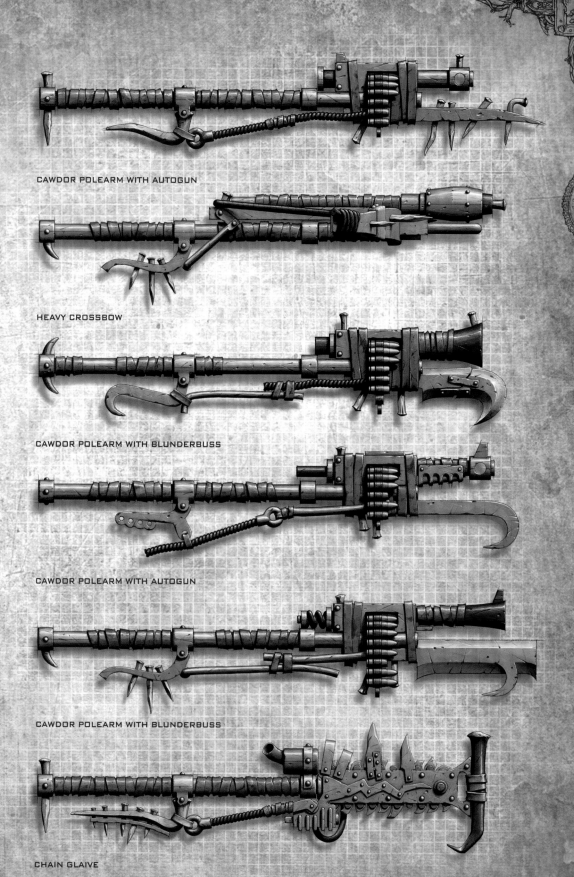

CAWDOR POLEARM WITH AUTOGUN

HEAVY CROSSBOW

CAWDOR POLEARM WITH BLUNDERBUSS

CAWDOR POLEARM WITH AUTOGUN

CAWDOR POLEARM WITH BLUNDERBUSS

CHAIN GLAIVE

HORATH THE SOULLESS
SUMPTOWN WRAITHS
HOUSE DELAQUE

GANGS OF HOUSE DELAQUE

There is something very unsettling about the Delaque, something that makes the skin of honest (and even dishonest) citizens crawl. While other Clan Houses proudly proclaim their strengths, screaming their dominance to all who will listen, Delaque silently waits and watches, leaving others to wonder what dark thoughts the House of Secrets harbours.

Many myths surround the Delaque, though it is widely known that long ago the House sold its soul to Lord Helmawr in exchange for a special place among his servants. Acting as Lord Helmawr's eyes and ears below the Wall, they syphon information from those places and peoples beyond the reach of his more conventional agents. For a steady supply of information, the House enjoys trade contracts, desirable hive districts and off-world technologies. It is said that while the other clans struggle for the spoils of their world, House Delaque plays a larger game – its sights firmly set upon joining the ranks of the Noble Houses. Of course, all of this is a story told by the Delaque themselves, and so is more than likely a lie.

The truth is that the stream of secrets flows not upwards, towards the Imperial House, but in the other direction. Long ago, the House uncovered a great and terrible truth of the Helmawr line, something buried by centuries of revisionist histories and the shifting ash of Necromunda. Wise and cunning even then, the masters of Delaque secured this secret before showing their hand to the Imperial House, shattering its truths into fragments and hiding them across the face of Necromunda. Unable to extinguish the upstarts without bringing this terrible secret to light, Helmawr instead struck a deal to bestow his favour upon the Delaque, even as he continued to wage a shadow war against them. And yet, for all of the grains of truth found within these tales, they are mined from a well of falsehoods, and so this too is likely a lie.

In reality, the Delaque hold their position not through their skill as spies, nor because of ancient debts unpaid, but because they are something far stranger than any might imagine. Though indigenous life on Necromunda is all but extinguished, some say that there are things buried deep beneath the hives that have endured the destructive millennia of Mankind's occupation. It is whispered that the Delaque are in league with some of these creatures, or perhaps they are their descendants, having found a way to hide in plain sight among the interlopers to their world. It is a notion so outlandish that only the truly insane believe it, but of course, this does not mean that it is not true – which is just as the Delaque intend it, for if everything is possible, then everything is a lie.

The House and its gangs thrive upon these dark rumours and tales, using falsehoods as a blade with which to carve up their enemies. Everything about them reinforces the use of obfuscation as both shield and sword, from the lenses that hide their eyes to the long cloaks that conceal an assassin's armoury of tools. Lined with holsters and hides, these long cloaks ensure a ganger is seldom without a blade or other weapon close to hand. A ganger's coat is also a mark of their status within the gang, and as they rise in rank and skill they will add more layers and linings to it. The oldest and most powerful among the Delaque are veritable magicians of war, the folds of their stormcoats hiding a murderous trinket for every occasion, each one available at the flick of a wrist.

The hideouts of a Delaque gang are as mysterious and evasive as the gangers themselves. Often locals won't even know that the silent strangers lurk in their midst. In the walls between domes, in the hidden and forgotten ducts that link hive levels, or beneath the creaking grated floors of hab markets, sometimes the signs of nomadic Delaque camps can be found. Always on the move, the gangs mark out their territories with obscure symbols, recognisable only to others of their house, each scrawled sign letting the Delaque know what to expect from locals, where goods might be scavenged or if secure boltholes are nearby. To a Delaque gang, their territory is often everywhere and nowhere, the men and women that support them doing so unwittingly, thinking their goods are going to their masters when in fact they end up in the gang's deep pockets.

Understandably, the stories surrounding the most notorious Delaque gangs are often contradictory. Names change in the telling or are purposefully altered, and the gangs do much to spread rumours, claim responsibility for the deeds of others or discredit truthful accounts with layers upon layers of lies. Even among this tapestry of falsehood, some Delaque gangs and their leaders are infamous enough to shine through, like pinpricks of light piercing the hive gloom. Eos 'Three-Nails', and the bloody left-handed palm print left upon Eos' victims, is a trademark recognised from the mercantile domes of Hive Primus to the corpse halls of Hive Mortis. Missing two of

WYRD ROULETTE –
A COMMON GAME OF CHANCE IN DELAQUE
OWNED GAMBLING DENS

its five fingers, the gory mark, with its distinctive overgrown nails and scarred palm print, is often the only evidence of the assassin's work. That the Great Houses, clans and gangs believe Eos is a Delaque is often taken as a compliment by the house, though none among the Star Chamber have ever uttered the killer's name. Some believe Eos is not just one ganger and their gang but many, and that there is a secret Delaque cult of killers that carry around the severed hand of their founder – the real Eos having died long ago.

Information, misdirection and manipulation are as important to Delaque gangs as killing. In fact, those such as Nycthos and the Children of the Augur deal as much in secrets as they do in death. Of all of the info-brokers of Hive Arcopolis, Nycthos has cultivated a reputation for knowing just what needs to be known, and is always ready to trade if the price is right. It is said that the Hall of Lies, where truth will cost you, is run by Nycthos' gang. Certainly, those that cross the tale-peddlers or bring violence into the hall can find that their information turns bad – dark rumours leading them into danger or trusted allies turning on them because of mistruths.

The strangest of all the Delaque gangs to stalk the hive depths is without doubt the Covenant of Shadows. A collection of dead names and ancient deeds, the Covenant keeps alive the memory and infamy of the heroes of the House. Yeomag the Eyeless, the Ghost of Gothrul, and the Shiver Twins are just some of the personas donned by the gangs sworn to keep the Covenant. No matter where upon Necromunda the gang resides, or which masters it nominally pays tribute to, when the Covenant calls, they become the great gang leaders and warriors of old. So complete is this transformation, the gang members changing their personalities and even their faces, it is whispered that they are a cabal of psykers who literally channel the dead.

PHANTOM
THE ASH WALKERS
HOUSE DELAQUE

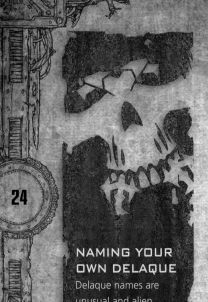

FIGHTERS

A starting Delaque gang is made up of the following fighters:

LEADER .... 110 CREDITS

M	WS	BS	S	T	W	I	A	Ld	Cl	Wil	Int
5"	3+	3+	3	3	2	3+	2	6+	6+	5+	6+

EQUIPMENT

A Delaque Leader is equipped with flak armour. They have no weapon restrictions.

STARTING SKILL

Delaque Leaders start with one free skill chosen from their Primary skill sets.

CHAMPIONS .... 95 CREDITS EACH

M	WS	BS	S	T	W	I	A	Ld	Cl	Wil	Int
5"	3+	3+	3	3	2	4+	2	7+	6+	6+	6+

EQUIPMENT

A Delaque Champion is equipped with flak armour. They have no weapon restrictions.

STARTING SKILL

Delaque Champions start with one free skill chosen from their Primary skill sets.

JUVES .... 25 CREDITS EACH

M	WS	BS	S	T	W	I	A	Ld	Cl	Wil	Int
6"	5+	5+	3	3	1	3+	1	9+	7+	8+	8+

EQUIPMENT

A Delaque Juve starts with no equipment. They can be armed with Pistols and Close Combat Weapons, but cannot be given any item that is worth more than 20 credits when they are added to the gang. During a campaign, once a Juve has gained their first Advancement, this limit no longer applies.

GANGERS .... 50 CREDITS EACH

M	WS	BS	S	T	W	I	A	Ld	Cl	Wil	Int
5"	4+	4+	3	3	1	4+	1	7+	6+	7+	7+

EQUIPMENT

A Delaque Ganger is equipped with flak armour. They can be armed with Basic Weapons, Close Combat Weapons and Pistols. When the gang is created, one Ganger can be armed with a Special Weapon. During a campaign, additional Gangers can also take Special Weapons as they are added.

SKILL ACCESS

Delaque fighters have access to the following skills.

	Agility	Brawn	Combat	Cunning	Ferocity	Leadership	Shooting	Savant
Leader	Primary	-	-	Primary	-	Primary	Secondary	Secondary
Champion	Secondary	-	-	Primary	-	Secondary	Primary	Secondary
Juve	Secondary	-	-	Primary	-	-	Secondary	-
Specialist	Secondary	-	Secondary	Primary	-	-	Primary	-

HOUSE DELAQUE EQUIPMENT LIST

WEAPONS
BASIC WEAPONS
- Autogun.................................... 15 credits
- Shotgun (with solid and scatter ammo).... 30 credits
- Lasgun.................................... 15 credits
- Throwing knives .... 10 credits

CLOSE COMBAT WEAPONS
- Digi lasers .... 25 credits
- Shock stave .... 25 credits
- Stiletto knife .... 20 credits
- Web gauntlet .... 35 credits

PISTOLS
- Autopistol................................ 5 credits
- Flechette pistol
  (with solid and fleshbane ammo) .... 30 credits
- Hand flamer .... 75 credits
- Laspistol .... 10 credits
- Plasma pistol............................. 50 credits
- Stub gun .... 5 credits
- Web pistol .... 80 credits

SPECIAL WEAPONS
- Flamer .... 140 credits
- Grav gun .... 120 credits
- Long rifle .... 30 credits
- Meltagun.................................. 135 credits
- Plasma gun................................ 100 credits
- Web gun .... 115 credits

HEAVY WEAPONS
- Heavy flamer* .... 195 credits

WARGEAR
GRENADES
- Choke gas grenades .... 50 credits
- Photon flash grenades .... 15 credits
- Scare gas grenades .... 40 credits
- Smoke grenades .... 15 credits
- Stun grenades .... 10 credits

ARMOUR
- Flak armour .... 10 credits
- Mesh armour............................... 15 credits

PERSONAL EQUIPMENT
- Bio-scanner............................... 30 credits
- Filter plugs.............................. 10 credits
- Grapnel launcher .... 25 credits
- Gunshroud .... 10 credits
- Infra sight[†]........................... 35 credits
- Mono-sight[†] .... 35 credits
- Photo-goggles .... 20 credits
- Respirator .... 15 credits
- Skinblade................................. 10 credits
- Web solvent .... 25 credits

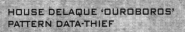
**HOUSE DELAQUE 'OUROBOROS'
PATTERN DATA-THIEF**

MIST STALKER
CHEAPSIDE SPEKTRES
HOUSE DELAQUE

HOUSE DELAQUE WEAPONRY

GRAV GUN

WEB GAUNTLET

HAND FLAMER

STUB GUN

LASPISTOL

AUTOPISTOL

SHOTGUN

AUTOGUN

FLECHETTE PISTOL

LONG RIFLE

JERRA THE STALKER
WYRD SISTERS
HOUSE ESCHER

GANGS OF HOUSE ESCHER

House Escher is unique among the great Houses of Necromunda for its gangs are entirely made up of women. Masters of pharmaceuticals and chemical manipulation, millennia of dabbling in potent alchemical technologies has left their men-folk as withered and imbecilic weaklings, good only for artificial breeding programs and gene-harvesting. The House regards this as no great deficiency and Escher gangers are among the most lethal to stalk the hives of Necromunda. What an Escher might lack in raw physical strength compared to a Goliath, she more than makes up for in speed, skill and sheer psychotic flare.

Escher gang leaders rise from the ranks of the House by virtue of their destructive attitudes and furious intelligence. Many of these hive war-maidens were once narco-terrorists, riot-girls or combat-chem test subjects. Too unhinged or aggressive for the House labs or trade clans, their skills have been turned to wreaking havoc on Escher's rivals amongst the other Clan Houses.

Like-minded Escher gangers will flock to the side of a powerful leader when she emerges, mirroring the politicking of the House's Matriarchal Council, as they yearn to be close to the most powerful of their kin. This can extend beyond a taste for shared homicide and mayhem, as Escher gangers mimic the style and fashions of their leader, though being careful never to overshadow her. Bedecked in cutting edge accoutrements and with distinctive and striking hair styles, an Escher gang could almost be mistaken for hive socialites, if it wasn't for the cold glares, manic grins and all of the guns.

Murder is a lifestyle choice for most Escher gangers and they gain little satisfaction from simply dispatching their enemies – though they are not adverse to a bullet in the skull or knife to the throat if it is called for. Speed, style and displays of merciless violence are the hallmarks of the Escher gang. Enemies are not merely killed; they are toyed with, crippled by blinding blade strikes, sent insane by hallucinogenic drugs or driven to their knees vomiting blood by vicious toxins. The showmanship of death is a prized trait among Eschers and the greatest of their gang leaders have hundreds of trophies to show for their killing sprees. Escher gangs often compete for the most callous or stylish murder, whether it is committed close in with blades and boots, delivered by bespoke venoms or with an expert shot placed for the most visceral effect.

As befits the character of their parent Clan House, Escher gangs make extensive use of especially tailored chemicals and elixirs, both on themselves and their enemies. On weapons this can include envenomed blades, concealed drug-injectors and the much-feared chem-throwers. In combat, these can swiftly dispatch foes with a slightest cut or exploit a gap in their defences, reaching targets who foolishly

considered themselves safe. On a macro level, Escher gangs have been known to flood entire hab zones with psychotropic gas, turning the battlefield into a madhouse for their debilitated foes as Escher fighters run and dance among them, gifting slaughter with every gesture.

Escher gangs have a well-deserved reputation for cruelty, even by the callous standards of Necromunda. Fallen foes can expect no mercy, and putting an extra round or two into a corpse is considered standard practise for most of their gangers – and woe to any that find themselves taken prisoner. The lucky ones might hope to be bartered back to their brethren quickly and with a minimum of permanent damage done. The less fortunate become test subjects for the gang's pharmaceutical experimentation or target practise on their training range.

Escher gangs do not make their hideouts in the shadows like many other hive gangs. Even those with dark reputations and hefty bounties on their heads often flaunt the protection of their House by moving about among their 'betters'. Many upscale establishments such as spire-ward hallucinatoriums, chemfactor bordellos or companion-haunts are thinly veiled fronts for Escher activities. Here, among the decadent upper underclass and gaudy faux-nobility the gang holds court, spreading its influence out into the surrounding domes and hab zones. Many a hab-praefect or enforcer captain is the unwitting pawn of an Escher gang, manipulated by a dependence on bespoke elixirs and the promise of forbidden things only the gang can provide.

ESCHER HOOKAH
PHARMACEUTICAL UNIT

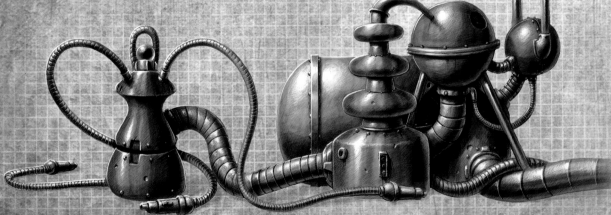

Legends of powerful and influential Escher gangs abound among the hives of Necromunda. Such tales are often spoken with a tone of awe and fear, as if the recounting of such deeds might infect the teller, or their listeners, with some measure of the Escher's criminal insanity. Perhaps the most feared leader to rise from the Escher of Hive Temenos was Aryn Shivergloom. Clad in impossibly expensive off-world feathers and gaudy leathers she was the terror of the Red Thorn uprising and the architect of the Hab 23 dome collapse – an event that slew one of her rivals at the cost of ten thousand hapless workers. It is said none dared bar her way, for she killed without conscience, mercy or hesitation, especially those who annoyed her by doing unforgivable things – such as interrupting her incessant mumbling, walking on the wrong side of the street or stepping on her shadow.

Other leaders have also made their mark and left behind a dark legacy, such as Yolanda Vor who is attributed with perhaps the single most impressive kill of any Escher. After reading a proclamation made by the Arbiter General of Hive Trazior – that condemned her personally for various crimes – she strode into a high council meeting and drove a dagger through his eye. The resulting firefight and Yolanda's running gun battle to escape left scars throughout the council dome that have yet to be fully repaired. Then there are those Eschers that are truly myths – such as Gabriella Aves. After dominating the western wards of Hive Primus and piling high the heads of her enemies, she announced she craved a new and worthy challenge. Gathering up her gang she set off across the wastes for Hive Secundus. To this day tales filter back from those Ash Wasters bold enough to pass through the cursed hive, tales of a mighty warrior queen and her amazonian army.

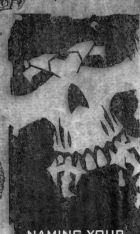

FIGHTERS

A starting Escher gang is made up of the following fighters:

LEADER .... 120 CREDITS

M	WS	BS	S	T	W	I	A	Ld	Cl	Wil	Int
5"	3+	3+	3	3	2	2+	3	5+	6+	6+	7+

EQUIPMENT

An Escher Leader is equipped with flak armour. They have no weapon restrictions.

STARTING SKILL

Escher Leaders start with one free skill chosen from their Primary skill sets.

CHAMPIONS .... 95 CREDITS EACH

M	WS	BS	S	T	W	I	A	Ld	Cl	Wil	Int
5"	3+	3+	3	3	2	2+	2	6+	7+	6+	6+

EQUIPMENT

An Escher Champion is equipped with flak armour. They have no weapon restrictions.

STARTING SKILL

Escher Champions start with one free skill chosen from their Primary skill sets.

JUVES .... 20 CREDITS EACH

M	WS	BS	S	T	W	I	A	Ld	Cl	Wil	Int
6"	4+	5+	2	3	1	2+	1	8+	9+	8+	8+

EQUIPMENT

An Escher Juve starts with no equipment. They can be armed with Pistols and Close Combat Weapons, but cannot be given any item that is worth more than 20 credits when they are added to the gang. During a campaign, once a Juve has gained their first Advancement, this limit no longer applies.

GANGERS .... 50 CREDITS EACH

M	WS	BS	S	T	W	I	A	Ld	Cl	Wil	Int
5"	4+	4+	3	3	1	3+	1	7+	8+	7+	7+

EQUIPMENT

An Escher Ganger is equipped with flak armour. They can be armed with Basic Weapons, Close Combat Weapons and Pistols. When the gang is created, one Ganger can be armed with a Special Weapon. During a campaign, additional Gangers can also take Special Weapons as they are added.

NAMING YOUR OWN ESCHERS

Escher names often come from great heroes and hell raisers of the clan, carried by their new owners with pride and no small amount of swagger. Below are some names that can be used, adapted or combined when creating your own Escher gang.

- Jeliki
- Sakura
- Trix
- Elle
- Viata
- Nenrietta
- Anya
- Exene
- Lydial
- Niko
- Sioux
- Ava
- Gielle
- Candela
- Cyberna
- Alexa
- Iris
- Io
- Exa
- Ami
- Swan
- Morta
- Raven
- Violet
- Ophelia
- Lace
- Selene
- Fable
- Vega
- Rain
- Silver
- Poly
- Ramona

SKILL ACCESS

Escher fighters have access to the following skills.

	Agility	Brawn	Combat	Cunning	Ferocity	Leadership	Shooting	Savant
Leader	Primary	-	Primary	Secondary	Secondary	Primary	-	-
Champion	Primary	-	Primary	Secondary	Secondary	Secondary	-	-
Juve	Primary	-	Secondary	Secondary	-	-	-	-
Specialist	Primary	-	Primary	Secondary	Secondary	-	-	-

HOUSE ESCHER EQUIPMENT LIST

WEAPONS

BASIC WEAPONS
- Autogun.. 15 credits
- Lasgun... 5 credits
- Shotgun
  (with solid and scatter ammo).................. 30 credits

CLOSE COMBAT WEAPONS
- Chainsword.. 25 credits
- Fighting knife .... 15 credits
- Power knife .... 25 credits
- Power sword .... 45 credits
- Shock whip... 25 credits
- Stiletto knife.. 20 credits
- Stiletto sword....................................... 30 credits

PISTOLS
- Autopistol.. 10 credits
- Hand flamer .... 75 credits
- Laspistol .... 10 credits
- Needle pistol.. 25 credits
- Plasma pistol.. 50 credits
- Stub gun .... 5 credits

SPECIAL WEAPONS
- Combi-weapon (bolter/needler) .... 80 credits
- Flamer .... 140 credits
- Meltagun... 135 credits
- Needle rifle .... 35 credits
- 'Nightshade' chem-thrower .... 135 credits
- Plasma gun.. 100 credits

HEAVY WEAPONS
- Heavy stubber..................................... 130 credits*

WARGEAR

GRENADES
- Choke gas grenades .... 45 credits
- Frag grenades.. 30 credits
- Krak grenades .... 45 credits
- Photon flash grenades .... 15 credits
- Scare gas grenades .... 40 credits
- Smoke grenades .... 15 credits

ARMOUR
- Flak armour .... 10 credits
- Mesh armour... 15 credits

PERSONAL EQUIPMENT
- Acid rounds (for shotgun)....................... 15 credits
- Chem-synth.. 15 credits
- Drop rig... 10 credits
- Dumdum rounds (for stub gun) .... 5 credits
- Filter plugs.. 10 credits
- Las-projector... 35 credits
- Photo goggles .... 35 credits
- Respirator .... 15 credits

'CUT-UP' RYNNE
HELL'S OWN
HOUSE ESCHER

HOUSE ESCHER WEAPONRY

LASPISTOL

AUTOPISTOL

CHOKE GAS GRENADE

STUB GUN

STILETTO KNIFE

COMBI-BOLTER/NEEDLER

STILETTO SWORD

MELTAGUN

PLASMA GUN

CHAINSWORD

34

PLASMA PISTOL

HAND FLAMER

NEEDLE RIFLE

FLAMER

LASGUN

AUTOGUN

SHOTGUN

HEAVY STUBBER

BROK THE STIMMER
SHIV'S CRUSHERS
HOUSE GOLIATH

GANGS OF HOUSE GOLIATH

The gangers that fight in the name of House Goliath are hulking brutes, each a pillar of muscle and pent-up violence ready to be unleashed. These massive warriors are the product of House Goliath work-clans, each of them gene-smithed using stim-elixirs traded from House Escher for a life of punishing labour and hardship in the depths of the house's foundries and refineries. Far larger and stronger than an ordinary human, they flaunt their strength wherever they go, and it is difficult to ignore the air of brutality Goliaths wear like a mantle. However, their genetic gifts come with a price, for the forge that burns twice as hot only burns half as long, resulting in a drastically shortened lifespan – even by the dismal standards of Necromunda.

Membership in a gang offers a Goliath a life beyond the foundry and a chance for greatness – not to mention the opportunity to crack some skulls. When a charismatic and cunning leader emerges from among the work crews the House masters are quick to make their offer. Intelligence and initiative – traits that are of little value in the foundries are then put to good use against rival Houses. Such leaders are provided weapons and armour – often adapted from factory tools and protective gear – and allowed the pick of their crew. The new gang is then turned out, its battle-hungry leader needing little prompting to go forth and find trouble.

House Goliath retains a measure of control over the gang through the chem-leash each ganger wears about their neck. All Goliaths need a steady supply of chems and stims to keep their massive bodies functioning and to provide them with their impressive strength. It is a rare cocktail controlled by the House masters, and one they use to keep the gangs and work clans in line. Each ganger wears about their person one or more auto-rigs that regulate the delivery of these stims into their bloodstream, and while a ganger can go some time between hits – provided they conserve their strength – eventually they will exhaust their supply and will need what only the House can provide lest their short lives become even shorter or worse, their bodies erupt in sudden and uncontrolled growth. Despite this, rumours persist of Goliath gangs gone rogue, having replaced their dependence with black-market remedies, xenos drugs or even the flesh of the dead.

Goliath gangs are about as subtle as a fist to the face when it comes to fighting. Fancy tactics and sneaky ambushes are the tools of the weak, and a Goliath will seldom stoop to such lows. Goliath gangers favour closing with the enemy as quickly as possible, grabbing them by the throat and not letting go until either the ganger or the foe is lying on the ground screaming out their last breath. For fighters lacking the strength and resilience of a Goliath, such tactics would doubtless be suicide, their puny bodies broken by gunfire or grenades as soon as they left cover. A Goliath however has the stamina to see it through, and the stoicism – perhaps the result of their shortened lifespan – to accept death should they fail.

Goliath leaders embody these shock and awe techniques and are often the first into the fray, roaring like a bull-grox and waving for their gang to follow. It is a matter of pride for a Goliath leader to personally break the opposing gang leader, or at very least perpetrate some act of extreme violence, such as ripping off an enemy's head or punching their teeth out of the back of their skull in full view of their gang.

The weapons favoured by Goliath gangs reflect their up-close-and-personal tactics, generally focusing on short range firepower, guns with large magazines and high rates of fire or hefty melee weapons selected as much for their fearsome appearance as the damage they can inflict. In fact, most Goliath ranged weapons and gear can be pressed into service for close up combat. Lasguns and autoguns are constructed to be heavy and blunt, while pistols have weighted handles, all the better for breaking bones. Armour plates and studs on armour and clothing serve a similar purpose, turning every bit of a Goliath's body into a crude but lethal weapon when propelled by their mighty thews.

The domain of a Goliath gang is often deep in the heart of an abandoned slagheap, rad-cursed abandoned manufactory or sump forge. These forsaken places are toxic to those without the Goliath's gene-smithed gifts and the harsh environment seems to remind them of home. Goliaths gladly endure these hardships for they reinforce the cherished belief that the other Clan Houses are populated with weaklings. These hideouts are also often filled with a wealth of cast-off scrap that can be used to support the gang's growing arsenal. Over time they might grow into settlements in their own right as the gang puts their industrial skills to work creating heavy equipment, homemade weaponry and makeshift armour.

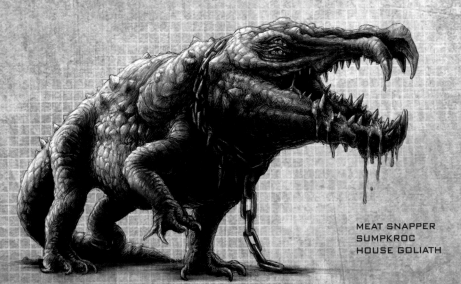

MEAT SNAPPER
SUMPKROC
HOUSE GOLIATH

Goliaths will trade with other gangs for what they need, most notably technological items or drugs they cannot manufacture themselves, but playing merchant is not what they are best at – they tend to make deals based on the threat of sudden and brutal violence rather than any kind of trader's acumen. More likely, the gang will simply take what it needs, as this fits better with their belief that strength is all. Wise hive traders know that if you intend to treat with a Goliath gang you had best be ready to prove your willingness to fight, at least if you want to strike a good deal.

The hives of Necromunda are filled with countless notorious Goliath gangs and some of the greatest acts of inter-House warfare can be attributed to them. Durgan Kill-Fist and his 'Knuckle Boys' once turned an entire hab-dome into their own personal pit fight. Welding the blast doors and conveyors shut, they trapped three rival gangs before sparking a brawl that dragged on for three days, painting the tunnels red with blood. Gurnark the Bootking held the great West Ashgate of Hive Acropolis for a whole month. His gangers terrorized the local merchants, demanding tribute for passage and turning their stubber turrets on anyone not quick enough to bend the knee to the Bootking. Though few live long enough, it is the dream of many Goliaths to ascend the hive and join the ranks of the House masters. One who did so is Hectork Scrak, whose dark deeds are only whispered of, even if his massive girth makes his genetic history unmistakable.

'PROMETHIUM' VINN
STEEL BRUTES
HOUSE GOLIATH

NAMING YOUR OWN GOLIATHS

Goliath names are simple and brutal, just like the gangers themselves, and are also easy to yell out in the midst of a firefight or when charging down enemies. Below are some names that can be used, adapted or combined when creating your own Goliath gang.

- King
- Orman
- Gund
- Hagen
- Logan
- Spike
- Gunk
- Stubber
- Punker
- Ghork
- Ukak
- Vorg
- Blitz
- Grand Dog
- Skullsmasher
- Dead'ead
- Bonesnapper

FIGHTERS

A starting Goliath gang is made up of the following fighters:

LEADER .... 145 CREDITS

M	WS	BS	S	T	W	I	A	Ld	Cl	Wil	Int
4"	3+	3+	4	4	2	3+	3	5+	4+	8+	7+

EQUIPMENT

A Goliath Leader is equipped with furnace plate armour. They have no weapon restrictions.

STARTING SKILL

Goliath Leaders start with one free skill chosen from their Primary skill sets.

CHAMPIONS .... 110 CREDITS EACH

M	WS	BS	S	T	W	I	A	Ld	Cl	Wil	Int
4"	3+	4+	4	4	2	4+	2	6+	5+	8+	8+

EQUIPMENT

A Goliath Champion is equipped with furnace plate armour. They have no weapon restrictions.

STARTING SKILL

Goliath Champions start with one free skill chosen from their Primary skill sets.

JUVES .... 25 CREDITS EACH

M	WS	BS	S	T	W	I	A	Ld	Cl	Wil	Int
5"	4+	5+	3	3	1	3+	1	9+	5+	10+	9+

EQUIPMENT

A Goliath Juve starts with no equipment. They can be armed with Pistols and Close Combat Weapons, but cannot be given any item that is worth more than 20 credits when they are added to the gang. During a campaign, once a Juve has gained their first Advancement, this limit no longer applies.

GANGERS .... 60 CREDITS EACH

M	WS	BS	S	T	W	I	A	Ld	Cl	Wil	Int
4"	4+	4+	4	4	1	4+	1	8+	5+	9+	8+

EQUIPMENT

A Goliath Ganger is equipped with furnace plate armour. They can be armed with Basic Weapons, Close Combat Weapons and Pistols. When the gang is created, one Ganger can be armed with a Special Weapon. During a campaign, additional Gangers can also take Special Weapons as they are added.

SKILL ACCESS

Goliath fighters have access to the following skills.

	Agility	Brawn	Combat	Cunning	Ferocity	Leadership	Shooting	Savant
Leader	-	Primary	Secondary	-	Primary	Primary	Secondary	-
Champion	-	Primary	Secondary	-	Primary	Secondary	Secondary	-
Juve	Secondary	Secondary	-	-	Primary	-	-	-
Specialist	-	Primary	Secondary	-	Primary	-	Secondary	-

HOUSE GOLIATH EQUIPMENT LIST

WEAPONS

BASIC WEAPONS
- Boltgun .... 55 credits
- Combat shotgun
  (with salvo & shredder ammo) .... 60 credits
- Shotgun (with solid & scatter ammo) .... 30 credits
- Stub cannon .... 20 credits

CLOSE COMBAT WEAPONS
- Axe.. 10 credits
- Brute cleaver... 20 credits
- Chainsword .... 25 credits
- Fighting knife .... 10 credits
- Maul (club) .... 10 credits
- Power axe.. 35 credits
- Power hammer .... 45 credits
- 'Renderizer' serrated axe*...................... 40 credits
- Spud-jacker .... 15 credits
- Two-handed axe* .... 25 credits
- Two-handed hammer* .... 35 credits

PISTOLS
- Combi-pistol (stub gun/plasma pistol) ...... 40 credits
- Bolt pistol .... 45 credits
- Hand flamer .... 75 credits
- Stub gun .... 5 credits

SPECIAL WEAPONS
- Combi-weapon (bolter/flamer)............... 175 credits
- Combi-weapon (bolter/melta) .... 165 credits
- Flamer .... 140 credits
- Grenade launcher
  (with frag & krak grenades) .... 55 credits
- Meltagun... 135 credits

HEAVY WEAPONS
- Heavy bolter* .... 160 credits
- Heavy flamer* .... 195 credits
- Heavy stubber*..................................... 130 credits
- 'Krumper' rivet cannon*......................... 70 credits

WARGEAR

GRENADES
- Blasting charges...................................... 35 credits
- Frag grenades... 30 credits
- Krak grenades .... 45 credits
- Smoke grenades .... 15 credits

ARMOUR
- Furnace plates .... 10 credits

PERSONAL EQUIPMENT
- Bio-booster... 35 credits
- Drop rig.. 10 credits
- Dumdum rounds (for stub gun) .... 5 credits
- Photo-goggles .... 35 credits
- Respirator .... 15 credits
- Stimm-slug stash .... 25 credits

'SPIKE' BORGON
DOG SOLDIERS
HOUSE GOLIATH

HOUSE GOLIATH WEAPONRY

HAND FLAMER

STUB GUN

BOLT PISTOL

COMBAT SHOTGUN

COMBI-PISTOL
(STUB GUN/PLASMA PISTOL)

COMBI-BOLTER/MELTA

BOLTGUN

SHOTGUN

COMBI-BOLTER/FLAMER

HEAVY STUBBER

STUB CANNON

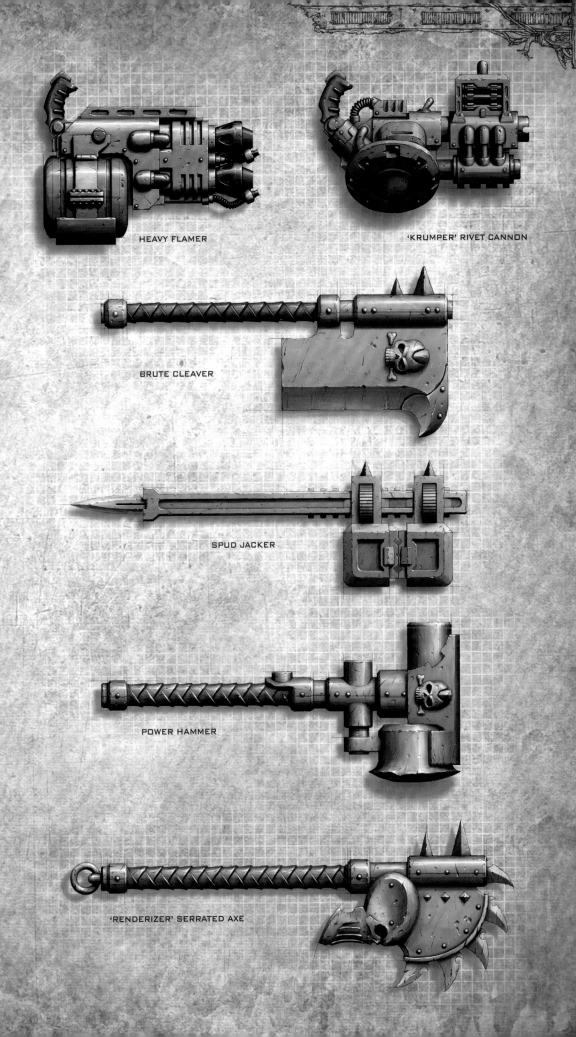

HEAVY FLAMER

'KRUMPER' RIVET CANNON

43

BRUTE CLEAVER

SPUD JACKER

POWER HAMMER

'RENDERIZER' SERRATED AXE

SHOTGUN JACK
SUMP DOGS
HOUSE ORLOCK

GANGS OF HOUSE ORLOCK

House Orlock is known throughout Necromunda as the 'House of Iron', an industrial superpower fuelled by countless ore mines and a stranglehold monopoly of the convoys serving the ferrous slagheaps that lie out in the Ash Wastes. To the other Houses of Necromunda, Orlock seems as unified as a clenched fist, its gangers well-organised, equipped and utterly united in purpose. Life for the average serf of House Orlock is one of unending servitude, with each man and woman doomed to endless toil within the cramped confines of the ore pits and mines from which their masters derive their vast wealth. All thought of rebellion among the masses is purged from the herd by stony-faced overseers at the cracking tip of electro-goad and psi-whip, until nought but unthinking obedience remains. Compared to these bent-backed serfs, the men and women of Orlock's gangs walk proud and tall through the smoke-clogged hallways of the House of Iron. To be an Orlock ganger is to have risen above the brutal drudgery of serfdom and claimed a life of violence and personal freedom in its stead. These are warriors born out of the fires of a vicious internal war, spoken of by the Orlocks as the 'Crucible Schism'.

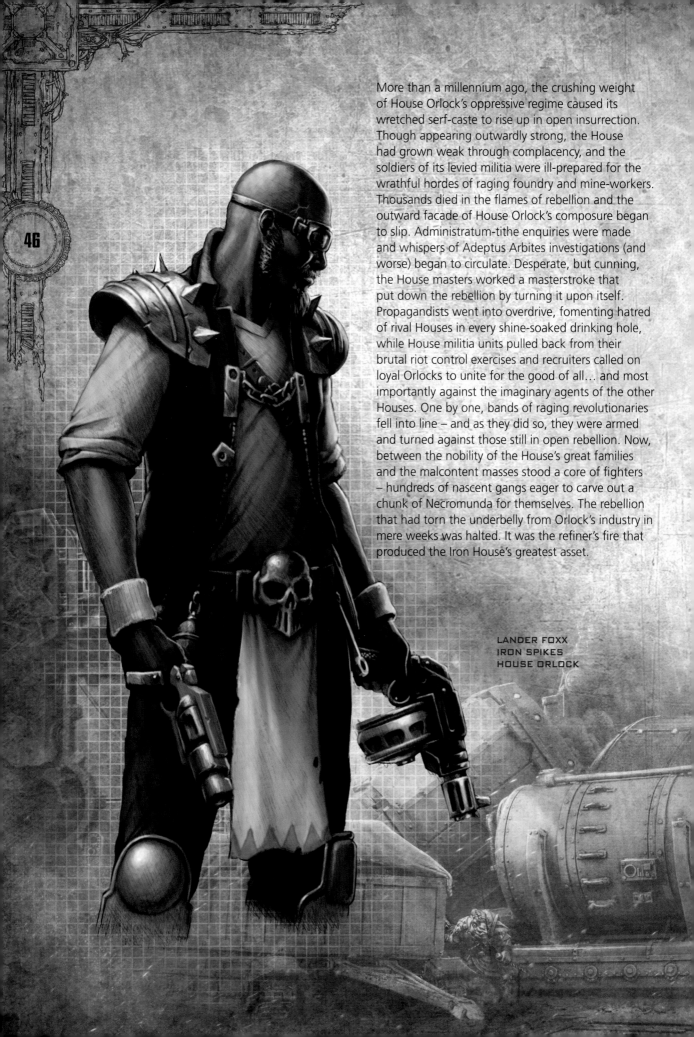

More than a millennium ago, the crushing weight of House Orlock's oppressive regime caused its wretched serf-caste to rise up in open insurrection. Though appearing outwardly strong, the House had grown weak through complacency, and the soldiers of its levied militia were ill-prepared for the wrathful hordes of raging foundry and mine-workers. Thousands died in the flames of rebellion and the outward facade of House Orlock's composure began to slip. Administratum-tithe enquiries were made and whispers of Adeptus Arbites investigations (and worse) began to circulate. Desperate, but cunning, the House masters worked a masterstroke that put down the rebellion by turning it upon itself. Propagandists went into overdrive, fomenting hatred of rival Houses in every shine-soaked drinking hole, while House militia units pulled back from their brutal riot control exercises and recruiters called on loyal Orlocks to unite for the good of all… and most importantly against the imaginary agents of the other Houses. One by one, bands of raging revolutionaries fell into line – and as they did so, they were armed and turned against those still in open rebellion. Now, between the nobility of the House's great families and the malcontent masses stood a core of fighters – hundreds of nascent gangs eager to carve out a chunk of Necromunda for themselves. The rebellion that had torn the underbelly from Orlock's industry in mere weeks was halted. It was the refiner's fire that produced the Iron House's greatest asset.

LANDER FOXX
IRON SPIKES
HOUSE ORLOCK

The relationship formed in the aftermath of the Crucible Schism remains in place centuries later. Every Orlock, no matter how lowly, looks to the gangers who saunter arrogantly among them with a mixture of envy, longing and fear. The gangs keep the masses in check, not merely by threat of violence, but through the hope of a better future – the 'nod' from a gang leader is the promise of a new life, away from electro-flails and endless toil. The role of the gangs stretches far beyond this basic perk, however, for they are the mailed fist of House Orlock in the constant skirmishes between the great Houses of Necromunda. They protect the vast ore convoys that ply the Ash Wastes as guards and outriders, ward off prying eyes from the monstrous slag deposits at hive-bottom, and patrol the dark tunnels that lead into rival territory.

Life in an Orlock gang is tough, for their warriors have none of the stimm-grown muscle of Goliath gangers, the murder-tech of House Van Saar or the poisons of the Escher. Instead, they rely on sturdy weapons stamped and pressed in the Orlock foundries, and a fighting spirit born from the House's us-against-them philosophy. In the drinking dens and gang houses of Orlock, every ganger is instilled with the warrior creed known as 'The Iron Brotherhood'. Put simply: my gang before my House, my House before the rest. This code is the way of life for every Orlock ganger, from the greenest Juve scalped from an ore-scraping line to the oldest Iron-touched shot-caller ready to head up-hive. Forget the code and a ganger ends up gutted, facedown in a sump-flow. Honour it, and their brothers and sisters will fight and die by their side.

This close-knit bond lends itself well to the Orlock methods of gang war. Orlocks pass openly through society, confident that their gang-kin have their backs at every turn. They carry sturdy autoguns, shotguns and stubbers, House-made and true-stamped. Reliability is sought after before all other factors, and it's said among the Orlocks that if a weapon doesn't spit lead stoppage-free, there's no place for it in the House of Iron – not that an Orlock won't take a trophy from a dead enemy, however. The irony of slaughtering a rival ganger with a weapon scavenged from the fallen has a poetry not lost on an Orlock's soul. With a ready supply of House-wrought weapons and munitions churned out by the House serfs, Orlock gangs are well-equipped to guard their territory. To do this, gangs typically form a network of 'friends' and accomplices who will warn them of encroachments onto their territories. This creates a loyalty among the local House serfs, who know that the loot plundered by the gangs will filter down to them, and they can expect first pickings after the gangers themselves.

Every Orlock gang has its own idiosyncrasies and traditions, but many style themselves after the notorious Iron Skulls, a sprawling gang who rose up in the wake of the Crucible Schism. The founder of the Iron Skulls was once a down-hive slag miner known as Cheros Jal. Jal's warriors carved out territory bordering with the Delaques in Hive Trazior over the course of several years and their actions helped foment the bitter rivalry with House Delaque that remains to this day.

Jal's greatest fame stems from the 'Ashline Heist', during which he and his outriders captured a Delaque armoured train and used it to smash apart the clan's grand pipeline nexus. The Delaque power in Trazior faded and House Orlock was able to wrest the much-coveted Ulanti contract from them. For three decades thereafter, Jal and his Iron Skulls ruled a swathe of Trazior that was the envy of all around them. Hounded at every turn by the murder-squads of House Delaque, the Iron Skulls became masters of ambush, maintaining a constant state of readiness that leaves them credited with the 'full fist' principle – no Orlock ganger travels alone, or without a gun in their hand. Jal's final fate is unknown. Some say he died outnumbered, fighting beside his crew, others that he wandered grey-haired and old into the Ash Wastes to seek their fate. Regardless, even now, Orlock gangers still speak of him in awed tones and many look to the Iron Skulls as the exemplars of what it means to be a ganger in the House of Iron.

'GUNNER' SKI
SUMP DOGS
HOUSE ORLOCK

FIGHTERS

A starting Orlock gang is made up of the following fighters:

LEADER .... 120 CREDITS

M	WS	BS	S	T	W	I	A	Ld	Cl	Wil	Int
5"	3+	3+	3	3	3	4+	2	4+	5+	5+	5+

EQUIPMENT
An Orlock Leader is equipped with mesh armour. They have no weapon restrictions.

STARTING SKILL
Orlock Leaders start with one free skill chosen from their Primary skill sets.

CHAMPIONS .... 95 CREDITS EACH

M	WS	BS	S	T	W	I	A	Ld	Cl	Wil	Int
5"	4+	3+	3	3	2	4+	2	5+	6+	6+	6+

EQUIPMENT
An Orlock Champion is equipped with mesh armour. They have no weapon restrictions.

STARTING SKILL
Orlock Champions start with one free skill chosen from their Primary skill sets.

JUVES .... 30 CREDITS EACH

M	WS	BS	S	T	W	I	A	Ld	Cl	Wil	Int
6"	5+	5+	3	3	1	3+	1	7+	8+	8+	8+

EQUIPMENT
An Orlock Juve starts with no equipment. They can be armed with Pistols and Close Combat Weapons, but cannot be given any item that is worth more than 20 credits when they are added to the gang. During a campaign, once a Juve has gained their first Advancement, this limit no longer applies.

GANGERS .... 55 CREDITS EACH

M	WS	BS	S	T	W	I	A	Ld	Cl	Wil	Int
5"	4+	4+	3	3	1	4+	1	6+	7+	7+	7+

EQUIPMENT
An Orlock Ganger is equipped with mesh armour. They can be armed with Basic Weapons, Close Combat Weapons and Pistols. When the gang is created, one Ganger can be armed with a Special Weapon. During a campaign, additional Gangers can also take Special Weapons as they are added.

SKILL ACCESS

Orlock fighters have access to the following skills.

	Agility	Brawn	Combat	Cunning	Ferocity	Leadership	Shooting	Savant
Leader	-	Secondary	-	-	Primary	Primary	Secondary	Primary
Champion	-	Secondary	-	-	Primary	Secondary	Secondary	Primary
Juve	-	-	-	-	Primary	-	Secondary	Secondary
Specialist	-	Secondary	-	-	Primary	-	Secondary	Primary

HOUSE ORLOCK EQUIPMENT LIST

WEAPONS

BASIC WEAPONS
- Autogun.. 15 credits
- Boltgun .... 55 credits
- Combat shotgun
  (with salvo & shredder ammo) .... 55 credits
- Sawn-off shotgun................................. 15 credits
- Shotgun (with solid & scatter ammo) ...... 25 credits

CLOSE COMBAT WEAPONS
- Chainsword...................................... 25 credits
- Fighting knife .... 15 credits
- Flail.. 20 credits
- Maul (club) .... 10 credits
- Power knife .... 25 credits
- Servo claw.. 30 credits
- Two-handed hammer* .... 35 credits

PISTOLS
- Autopistol....................................... 10 credits
- Bolt pistol .... 45 credits
- Hand flamer .... 75 credits
- Plasma pistol.................................... 50 credits
- Stub gun .... 5 credits

SPECIAL WEAPONS
- Combi-weapon (bolter/melta)............... 165 credits
- Flamer .... 140 credits
- Grenade launcher
  (with frag & krak grenades) .... 65 credits
- Plasma gun...................................... 100 credits
- Meltagun... 135 credits

HEAVY WEAPONS
- Harpoon launcher*............................. 110 credits
- Heavy bolter* .... 160 credits
- Heavy flamer* .... 195 credits
- Heavy stubber*.................................. 130 credits

WARGEAR

GRENADES
- Blasting charges.. 30 credits
- Demo charges .... 45 credits
- Frag grenades... 30 credits
- Krak grenades .... 45 credits

ARMOUR
- Flak armour .... 10 credits
- Mesh armour.. 15 credits

PERSONAL EQUIPMENT
- Bio-booster.. 35 credits
- Drop rig .... 10 credits
- Dumdum rounds (for stub gun) .... 5 credits
- Filter plugs.. 10 credits
- Photo-goggles .... 35 credits
- Respirator.. 15 credits
- Telescopic sight[†].................................... 25 credits

OLD JON GREYSON
ASH RUNNERS
HOUSE ORLOCK

HOUSE ORLOCK WEAPONRY

FIGHTING KNIFE

AUTOPISTOL

STUB GUN

HEAVY STUBBER

AUTOGUN

HARPOON LAUNCHER

COMBAT SHOTGUN

HANNAK SEVEN
COLDFIRE CABAL
HOUSE VAN SAAR

GANGS OF HOUSE VAN SAAR

House Van Saar is the technological powerhouse of Necromunda, its artisans and armourers creating the finest weapons and wargear of all of the clans. Their power, however, is built around a dark secret unknown to outsiders and even many within the House. Generations ago, the forefathers of the House toiled in the depths of the hives, seeking the lost knowledge of ages past. What they uncovered was a fragment of an ancient Standard Template Construct system, and it was upon this device that the clan's fortunes were built. Even for the augmented techno-scriveners of the Van Saar, such a thing as an STC is difficult to understand, and, though potent, the artefact was incomplete – and worse, it was flawed.

The STC bled exotic energies into all of those who used it, and the upper cabals of the House were soon hopelessly irradiated – a price they gladly paid for the technological wonders that the STC produced. While it is the oldest and most powerful Van Saar that drink deepest from the STC's poisoned chalice, and so are the most wizened and withered of their kind – all within the House are affected by it in one fashion or another. By the time a Van Saar comes of age, their body has already been exposed to radiation far in excess of the norm – even for a toxic world such as Necromunda – and they must spend most of their time encased in specially crafted suits to regulate their ravaged organs and polluted blood.

Unlike other Houses, which often seek out dissidents and hyper-violent misfits to fight their endless inter-House wars, House Van Saar chooses its gang Leaders from master crafters, tech-scriveners, and cognus-scholars. These learned men and women are more than mere weapons to be used against their rivals, but also innovators and salvagers, creating and recovering technologies for the House's masters. Well-versed in the catechisms of tech and the prayers to the machine, they have an understanding of the Imperium's ancient machines second only to the servants of the Mechanicum. Often, their mission is to recover lost tech from the depths of a hive or the vaults of their rivals – each find adding to the clan's arsenal of advancements. The greatest of these gang masters might be honoured for their work with unique tech gifts from their House, or if they have done Van Saar a truly exceptional service may even have a weapon variant or device named after them – like the Gantic pattern plasma gun or the Haex scrambler.

The true grail for a Van Saar gang is to find the missing pieces of their STC, and perhaps reverse or stall its degenerative effects upon their people. For this prize, they will delve deep into the underhive or trek out into the Ash Wastes and beyond. So far little progress has been made, and the gangs still rely upon cocktails of chemicals from their injector rigs or blood purification implants to prolong their lives.

As befits the fighters of a House rich in mechanical resources, Van Saar gangs favour technological solutions to battlefield challenges. Like the chambers of a well-greased stub gun, the gang enters the fray with each warrior knowing their role. An overseer of combat, the gang leader directs their followers, luring the foe into killing grounds, feinting with skirmishers and probing with speculative fire. Enemies are often detected in halos of green light on bio-scanner screens or upon pict thieves long before they are aware of the Van Saar fighters' presence, while meticulously machined and maintained plasma pistols, las carbines and rad guns track their advance. To a

Van Saar fighter, a weapon is more than merely a tool with which to bring down rivals, but a gift from the great work conclaves of the House. Like a child, it is theirs to care for and maintain, the weapon's life given purpose in their willing hands. For this reason, the gangers rarely use scavenged weaponry or anything that has not been crafted by the gang itself. Even seemingly crude weaponry, such as clubs or knives, are works of art – handles perfectly weighted against heads, the hafts fitted with pneumatic compellers to enhance swing, or edges tipped with monofilament strands to make them impossibly sharp.

Van Saar gangs thrust into the war between the Houses must forsake ties to their former masters. While they remain as cogs in the great House Van Saar machine, the gangs are now part of its farthest extremities. As the inner workings of the House see to its continuation, so do the gangs bring about favourable outcomes beyond its auspices. Where a Van Saar gang takes root, its Leader will build their own machine temple. These shadow forges are a pale reflection of the fabricator vaults of the House itself, but compared to the bases of other gangs they sufficiently provide the Van Saar gangers with a ready-made place to fashion weapons, charge power packs or craft armour. In the centre of such a hideout, the leader's own weapons and armour stand sentinel, almost a blessed relic to the gang, whose machine spirit, like the leader, watches over their endeavours.

Van Saar gangs and their leaders pursue the purity of technology just as they chase the advancement of their House. Often, a leader will choose one of the mysterious disciplines of the machine to master, and in turn shape the kind of gang they lead. Arch-mechakin Luthrek, for example, seeks out the ancient wonders of the hives, his gang of plunderers well known among the shadow realms beneath Gothrul's Needle. Festooned with trinkets of power, Luthrek has amassed a wealth of knowledge about the founders of the Needle, and often turns his environment against his enemies by manipulating forgotten systems to do his bidding. During the three-way firefight to break open Gothrul's Founder's Vault, Luthrek reawakened the spirits of the hive diggers – mighty engines quiescent since the hive's construction – the resulting quakes crushing his rivals under a cascade of ancient steel and scrap.

In the quest to cure the curse of the STC, some Van Saar leaders have even taken to adapting their own bodies. Through mechanical and chemical means, Mareke of the Urdo Vitaegineers is the most accomplished of her kind, as evidenced by the complex subdermal filters that whirr and hiss beneath her flesh. Mareke seeks out not blessed cybernetics or techno-scrap like many of her kin, but the perfect combinations of human chemicals for her anti-rad elixirs and enhancement potions. For years, Mareke and her gang have plagued the barrens of the Quinspirus Cluster, often raiding the vaults of the Mortuarium for their stores of dead. Her greatest prize though remains elusive; the Escher gang leader Xenrian. The two warrior women play out their private war, as Xenrian seeks to slay Mareke with exotic poisons and the Van Saar covets the Escher's unique genetic make-up for her dark experiments.

No tale of the great gangs of Van Saar would be complete without mentioning the legend of Razor's Abomination. Razor was one of the clan's most talented cyber-chirurgeons, who ironically met a messy end on the edge of a Delaque whisper-blade. Before his demise, it is said that Razor had found a cure to the exotic radiation exposure that affects all Van Saar to some degree, and the Abomination is his only surviving test subject. Stories of this mythical warrior and the gang he leads have led many Van Saar gangs – not to mention countless others seeking profit and fame – to their doom in the hive depths. Yet the tales persist, and from time to time there will be a sighting of a Van Saar fighter, hail and proud, striding into battle wearing the tattered remnants of a survival suit like a badge of honour.

JEAN SARGEN
THE NEXUS NINES
HOUSE VAN SAAR

FIGHTERS

A starting Van Saar gang is made up of the following fighters:

LEADER...130 CREDITS

M	WS	BS	S	T	W	I	A	Ld	Cl	Wil	Int
4"	4+	2+	3	3	2	5+	2	4+	5+	5+	4+

EQUIPMENT
A Van Saar Leader is equipped with an armoured bodyglove. They have no weapon restrictions.

STARTING SKILL
Van Saar Leaders start with one free skill chosen from their Primary skill sets.

CHAMPIONS...110 CREDITS EACH

M	WS	BS	S	T	W	I	A	Ld	Cl	Wil	Int
4"	4+	2+	3	3	2	4+	1	5+	6+	6+	5+

EQUIPMENT
A Van Saar Champion is equipped with an armoured bodyglove. They have no weapon restrictions.

STARTING SKILL
Van Saar Champions start with one free skill chosen from their Primary skill sets.

JUVES...35 CREDITS EACH

M	WS	BS	S	T	W	I	A	Ld	Cl	Wil	Int
5"	5+	4+	3	3	1	4+	1	9+	8+	9+	7+

EQUIPMENT
A Van Saar Juve is equipped with an armoured bodyglove. They can be armed with Pistols and Close Combat Weapons, but cannot be given any item that is worth more than 20 credits when they are added to the gang. During a campaign, once a Juve has gained their first Advancement, this limit no longer applies.

GANGERS...65 CREDITS EACH

M	WS	BS	S	T	W	I	A	Ld	Cl	Wil	Int
4"	4+	3+	3	3	1	5+	1	6+	7+	7+	6+

EQUIPMENT
A Van Saar Ganger is equipped with an armoured bodyglove. They can be armed with Basic Weapons, Close Combat Weapons and Pistols. When the gang is created, one Ganger can be armed with a Special Weapon. During a campaign, additional Gangers can also take Special Weapons as they are added.

SKILL ACCESS

Van Saar fighters have access to the following skills.

	Agility	Brawn	Combat	Cunning	Ferocity	Leadership	Shooting	Savant
Leader	Secondary	-	-	Secondary	-	Primary	Primary	Primary
Champion	-	-	Secondary	Secondary	-	Secondary	Primary	Primary
Juve	Primary	-	-	-	-	-	Secondary	Secondary
Specialist	-	-	Secondary	Secondary	-	-	Primary	Primary

HOUSE VAN SAAR EQUIPMENT LIST

WEAPONS

BASIC WEAPONS
- Lasgun... 10 credits
- Las carbine .... 20 credits
- Suppression laser .... 40 credits

CLOSE COMBAT WEAPONS
- 'Hystrar' pattern energy shield .... 50 credits
- Power knife .... 25 credits
- Servo claw .... 30 credits
- Shock baton .... 30 credits
- Shock stave .... 25 credits

PISTOLS
- Hand flamer .... 75 credits
- Las pistol .... 5 credits
- Las sub-carbine...................................... 15 credits
- Plasma pistol.. 50 credits

SPECIAL WEAPONS
- Combi-weapon (lasgun/melta).............. 120 credits
- Combi-weapon (lasgun/plasma gun)....... 75 credits
- Flamer.. 140 credits
- Grav gun.. 120 credits
- Meltagun.. 135 credits
- Plasma gun... 100 credits
- Rad gun.. 100 credits

HEAVY WEAPONS
- Plasma cannon* .... 130 credits
- Multi-melta*... 180 credits
- Rad cannon* .... 130 credits

WARGEAR

GRENADES
- Frag grenades.. 30 credits
- Krak grenades .... 45 credits
- Rad grenades... 25 credits
- Smoke grenades..................................... 15 credits

ARMOUR
- Flak armour .... 10 credits
- Mesh armour.. 15 credits

PERSONAL EQUIPMENT
- Bio-booster.. 35 credits
- Drop rig... 10 credits
- Filter plugs... 10 credits
- Grav chute... 40 credits
- Infra-sight[†]... 40 credits
- Las-projector.. 35 credits
- Mono-sight[†] .... 35 credits
- Photo-goggles.. 35 credits
- Respirator .... 15 credits
- Suspensors .... 60 credits
- Telescopic sight[†].................................... 25 credits

MAX ALDONA
BROKEN BROTHERHOOD
HOUSE VAN SAAR

HOUSE VAN SAAR WEAPONRY

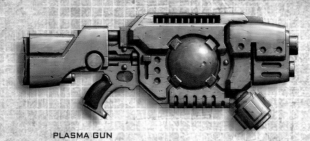

PLASMA GUN

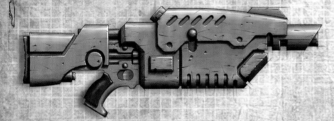

LAS CARBINE

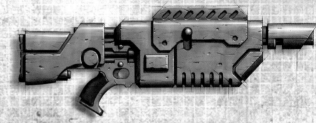

LASGUN

PLASMA PISTOL

LASPISTOL

COMBI-LASGUN/MELTA

RAD CANNON

ENERGY SHIELD

SHOCK STAVE AND SHOCK BATON

FRAG, KRAK AND RAD GRENADES

LARS LONGSHOT
BROKEN BROTHERHOOD
HOUSE VAN SAAR

HIRED GUNS

The Imperium of Man is a dangerous place. Countless billions of wretched souls deal with the bleakness of their existence by cowering from the horrors of the galaxy, dedicating their lives to relentless toil and drudgery in the service of Him on Earth.

Yet there are those who do not. Untold millions of brave or desperate souls take up arms, fighting for the fate of humanity in the Emperor's glorious armies. Many others, in numbers beyond counting, take to a life of violence for their own amusement, violent souls drawn to violent work. Yet more come to their bloody work through desperation, simply hoping to put food in their bellies. Ruthless bounty hunters prowl the underhive, hoping to get rich from their bloody-handed trade. Lowlife scum eke out a meagre existence, hiring their services to uncaring gang leaders looking for some expendable muscle. Even those who would prefer not to raise arms in violence find themselves drawn into the endless cycle of gang warfare, their skills retained in service of the crew that runs their hab block.

The hives of Necromunda are meat grinders for humanity. There is always someone willing to sell their services to keep the mechanism turning.

BOUNTY HUNTERS AND HIVE SCUM

In campaign play, gangs have the chance to recruit Hired Guns during the pre-battle sequence. This secures their services for that one battle. They are not added to the gang roster, but a Fighter card will need to be filled out for them. They can be hired again for subsequent battles – as such, players might find it useful to keep an appropriate Fighter card, already filled in, for each Hired Gun model they have.

Hired Guns never gain Experience, they cannot purchase Advancements, and they do not suffer Lasting Injuries – if they go Out of Action, they simply play no further part in the battle. Also, no additional equipment can be added to their Fighter card, aside from what is listed in their entry below.

In Skirmish battles, Hired Guns can be purchased in the same way as any other fighter.

In either mode of play, a Hired Gun increases the gang's Rating in the same way as any other fighter.

"Listen, stop struggling – your life's over… if they don't just stretch your neck, they're gonna ship you off to the slave-gangs. If you think downhive is hell, you ain't seen nothing yet."

Lodian Kreel,
Sanctioned
Bounty Hunter

HIVE SCUM...30 CREDITS

Hive Scum, or Scummers, are masterless or itinerant hivers who will fight for anyone who offers them coin. Many are drunkards and down-and-outs, but even these have their uses and, despite appearances, are quite capable of holding their own in a fight. Others are mercenaries who travel from zone to zone, making few friends or commitments, earning whatever easy money is around before moving on. Scum are too wild and independent to submit to the leadership of anyone for very long, and they hire out their services as they feel like it. Despite their carefree lifestyle and happy-go-lucky attitude, Scummers are good fighters, so their services are always in demand. Many end up working for the Guilders, but there are always a few willing to tag along with a gang for a share of the spoils.

Hive Scum are especially valuable to a newly-founded gang, especially one whose fighters may be neither numerous nor especially experienced. In general, more established gangs eschew their services, preferring to rely on their own in the heat of battle. Nonetheless, Hive Scum are considered of great value as cannon fodder…

A gang may recruit up to five Hive Scum at a time.

M	WS	BS	S	T	W	I	A	Ld	Cl	Wil	Int
5"	4+	4+	3	3	1	4+	1	8+	8+	8+	8+

EQUIPMENT

Hive Scum may purchase up to 60 credits' worth of weapons and Wargear from the Trading Post. They may take any Common item and may take any item with a Rarity value of 7 or below. The only weapons they may take are Pistols, Close Combat Weapons and Basic Weapons. They may be armed with up to three weapons, only one of which may have the Unwieldy Weapon Trait, and this counts as two weapons choices.

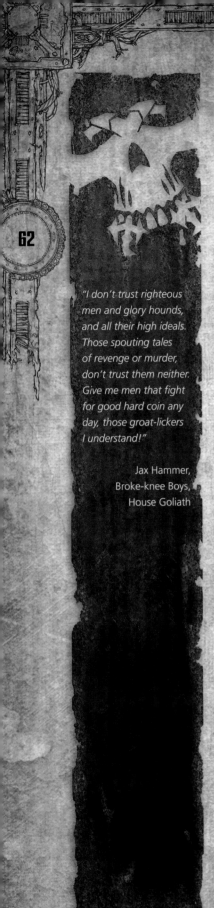

"I don't trust righteous men and glory hounds, and all their high ideals. Those spouting tales of revenge or murder, don't trust them neither. Give me men that fight for good hard coin any day, those groat-lickers I understand!"

Jax Hammer,
Broke-knee Boys,
House Goliath

BOUNTY HUNTERS..80 CREDITS

Bounty Hunters are amongst the toughest and most dangerous of all Necromunda underhivers. They survive in perilous conditions, living out in the wastes, pursuing outlaws and mutants through the tunnels and ruins. Bounty Hunters are loners who neither need, nor want, to be associated with a gang. They will hire their services to a gang leader, though, if there are no decent bounties to be had or if their interests are aligned, but such allegiances tend to be temporary.

Bounties are displayed at all Trading Posts, offering rewards to anyone who brings in outlaw leaders, gangs, mutants and other criminal types. Sometimes, general bounties are declared on Ratskin renegades or on underhive monsters. The rewards offered are good, but the job is a perilous one and many Bounty Hunters die out in the wastes, slain by the outlaws and mutants they set out to hunt.

Bounty Hunters are drawn from a wide range of backgrounds. Some are erstwhile gangers and might still bear some of the distinctive trappings of their former Clan House. Many Abhumans also find the life of a Bounty Hunter suits them well, for the Blood Warrant that serves as license and writ allows them to go where others of their kind might ordinarily be barred. Thus it is not uncommon to see Beastmen, Squats and other stable Abhuman strains operating as Bounty Hunters far from those areas set aside for their kind.

A gang can recruit no more than one Bounty Hunter at a time. To represent the great variety of Bounty Hunters active on Necromunda, the recruiting player picks one of the following profiles to use.

M	WS	BS	S	T	W	I	A	Ld	Cl	Wil	Int
5"	3+	3+	3	3	2	3+	1	7+	5+	6+	6+
3"	3+	4+	3	4	2	5+	1	5+	7+	5+	5+
4"	3+	4+	3	4	1	4+	2	7+	6+	7+	8+

EQUIPMENT

A Bounty Hunter is equipped with either mesh or flak armour. In addition, Bounty Hunters may purchase up to 150 credits' worth of weapons and Wargear from the Trading Post. They may take any Common item and may take any item with a Rarity value of 10 or below. They have no weapon restrictions. They may be armed with up to five weapons, only one of which may have the Unwieldy Weapon Trait, and this counts as two weapons choices.

SKILLS

A Bounty Hunter may take either three skills determined at random, or one skill determined at random and one skill chosen by the recruiting player. Each skill is chosen from the following skill sets: Agility, Brawn, Combat, Cunning, Ferocity, or Shooting. To determine a random skill, the player declares which skill set they are generating the skill from, and rolls a D6, re-rolling if the Bounty Hunter already has that skill. Choosing a skill is a simple matter of picking the desired skill from the sets available.

SPECIAL RULES

All Bounty Hunters, including named Dramatis Personae Bounty Hunters, benefit from the following special rules:

Dead, Not Alive: Any gang that employs a Bounty Hunter may be awarded extra bonuses for enemy fighters they help to bring down, due to the Bounty Hunter claiming extra fees from the authorities for troublesome gangers they bring in dead. In the post-battle sequence, when an opponent deletes a dead fighter from their roster during the Update Roster step of the post-battle sequence, the gang immediately claims half of that fighter's value, rounded up to the nearest 5 credits, as bounty.

Claiming Bounties: If the recruiting gang Captures an enemy fighter, roll a D6 in the Receive Rewards step of the post-battle sequence. On the roll of a 3 or higher, the Bounty Hunter recognises the Captive as a wanted outlaw. Mark this on the capturing gang's roster. If the Captive is later sold to the guilders, the Bounty Hunter receives an additional D6x10 credits.

"We'll Get Our Bit…": If a Bounty Hunter does not generate additional income during a campaign battle via the Dead, Not Alive or Claiming Bounties special rules above, there is a strong chance they will stick around until they do, whether the gang wants them to or not!

If, at the end of the Update Roster step of the post-battle sequence, only one of the Dead, Not Alive or Claiming Bounties special rules has been used, roll a D6. If the result is a 4 or higher, the Bounty Hunter is dissatisfied with their earnings and is available for the recruiting gang's next battle for free. If the result is a 1-3, they take their credits and leave.

If neither the Dead, Not Alive or Claiming Bounties special rules are used, there is no need to roll and the Bounty Hunter is automatically available for the recruiting gang's next battle for free.

If, however, both the Dead, Not Alive and Claiming Bounties special rules are used during the post-battle sequence, the Bounty Hunter, happy with their payment, automatically leaves.

If a Bounty Hunter that is available for the next battle for free in this way is not used, they will automatically leave. In other words, they must be used in the next battle, or be lost.

If a Bounty Hunter is taken Out of Action during a Campaign battle, they are considered to have automatically rolled a result of 12-26 – Out Cold on the Lasting Injuries table.

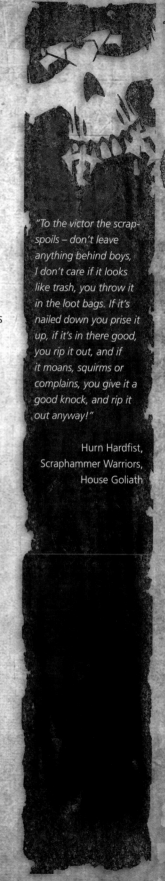

63

"To the victor the scrap-spoils – don't leave anything behind boys, I don't care if it looks like trash, you throw it in the loot bags. If it's nailed down you prise it up, if it's in there good, you rip it out, and if it moans, squirms or complains, you give it a good knock, and rip it out anyway!"

Hurn Hardfist,
Scraphammer Warriors,
House Goliath

BAERTRUM ARTUROS III, GUILDER BOUNTY HUNTER

Not all Bounty Hunters are desperados, loners or venators. Baertrum Arturos the Third is a member of the Adjurators, the Guilds' own private Order of hunters, concerned with the recovery of their own property and the reprimand of those responsible for taking it. Arturos and his kind operate primarily in the mid-hive regions, seeing to the interests of the mercantile lords and working to bring debtors and contract-breakers to justice. Sometimes, though, Adjurators might be required to venture into the underhive in search of their mark, bringing with them the special privileges and exceptional wargear afforded to a servant of the Guilds.

After running down a clan tithe-breaker, Arturos has remained in the underhive, having developed a taste for the fringe realm. He likes the way its denizens look to him with a mixture of fear and disgust reserved for their betters, while the rancid air and filthy surroundings reminds him that he was born of better stock than these bottom-feeders. While Arturos could make more scrip in the mid-hive domes, he couldn't throw his authority around quite as much. Despite his distaste for the denizens of the hive's lower reaches, he is not above allying himself with them when his interests and theirs are co-aligned. For the gangs' part, they hire Arturos because he is always cool-headed, quick with his needler and shrewd enough to avoid enemies getting the drop on him. That they have to put up with his perpetual scowls and condescending sneers, as well as his long, self-aggrandising diatribes, is a relatively small price to pay for such talents and the veneer of Guilder authority that comes with them.

BAERTRUM ARTUROS, BOUNTY HUNTER

290 CREDITS

M	WS	BS	S	T	W	I	A	Ld	Cl	Wil	Int
5"	3+	3+	3	3	2	3+	2	6+	5+	6+	5+

Weapon	Rng S	Rng L	Acc S	Acc L	Str	AP	D	Am	Traits
Artisan needle pistol with auto loader	4"	9"	+2	-	-	-1	-	4+	Sidearm, Silent, Toxin
Stiletto knife	-	E	-	-	-	-	-	-	Melee, Toxin

SKILLS: Disarm, Escape Artist, Nerves of Steel

WARGEAR: Infra-sight, light carapace armour

'All Gelt for the Guilders, and all Debts Paid in Full.'

Motto of the Adjurators Primus

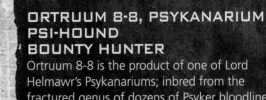

ORTRUUM 8-8, PSYKANARIUM PSI-HOUND
BOUNTY HUNTER

Ortruum 8-8 is the product of one of Lord Helmawr's Psykanariums; inbred from the fractured genus of dozens of Psyker bloodlines to create a horrifying, yet potent psychic weapon. Unable to stand or even feed itself, and of indeterminable gender, Ortruum 8-8's mutated form is augmented with suspensor implants to facilitate movement, inducer rigs to keep its organs functioning and a neural-crown that both enhances its psychic powers and keeps it in a docile and pliable state when required. Like most Psykanarium Bounty Hunters, Ortruum 8-8 is controlled by coded auditory and olfactory triggers, allowing its masters to direct it with a word or set it upon the scent of its prey.

ORTRUUM 8-8, BOUNTY HUNTER

250 CREDITS

M	WS	BS	S	T	W	I	A	Ld	Cl	Wil	Int
4"	5+	5+	3	3	2	4+	1	6+	7+	5+	5+

SKILLS: Fearsome, Sanctioned Psyker
SPECIAL RULES: Dead, Not Alive, Flight, Soul Hound, Team Work

WYRD POWERS:
TELEPATHY: Continuous Effect, Mind Lock (Basic), Premonition (Simple)
TELEKINESIS: Force Blast (Basic)

WYRD POWERS

TELEPATHY

PREMONITION (SIMPLE), CONTINUOUS EFFECT: The ability to read the thoughts of others possessed by this Psyker enables it to dodge and evade all but the most unexpected of attacks. This Wyrd Power grants the Psyker a 4+ save roll, which cannot be modified by a weapon's Armour Piercing characteristic.

MIND LOCK (BASIC): Nominate an enemy fighter anywhere within 18" of this Psyker that has not already activated this round. For the remainder of this round, that fighter cannot activate and may not take part in a group activation.

TELEKINESIS

FORCE BLAST (BASIC): Any enemy fighters within 3" of this Psyker are immediately pushed D3+1" directly away. If this movement would push a fighter from a platform or into a pitfall, stop at the edge and take an Initiative test for them. If the test is passed, they are placed Prone at the edge. If the test is failed, they will fall. If this movement is interrupted by a wall or other impassable terrain, the fighter is immediately Pinned and takes a hit with a Strength equal to the number of inches rolled for the push distance.

SPECIAL RULES

FLIGHT: Ortruum 8-8 ignores all terrain, may move freely between levels without restriction, and can never fall. It may not, however, ignore impassable terrain and may not end its movement with its base overlapping an obstacle or another fighter's base.

SOUL HOUND: A unique ability possessed by Ortruum 8-8, and one that makes its services particularly valuable to Bounty Hunters, Enforcers and Guilders, is the ability to hunt down individuals based on their psychic spoor. Before a game begins, nominate one fighter (Leader, Champion, Juve, Specialist or equivalent) from your opponent's gang. This fighter is the one that Ortruum 8-8 has been sent to track down. This fighter must be deployed on the table at the start of the game, and must therefore be included in your opponent's crew, however that is selected.

For the duration of this game, the nominated fighter is haloed by ghostly illumination, marking them out to their enemies as Ortruum 8-8 constantly focuses upon their location. All shooting attacks made against the nominated fighter gain a +1 modifier on hit rolls. Additionally, the nominated fighter may not use the Infiltrate or Lie Low skills for the duration of this game.

TEAM WORK: Ortruum 8-8 may be hired alongside other Bounty Hunters, allowing a gang to field two Bounty Hunters rather than the usual one.

HELMAWR'S PSYKERS

Psyker strains are carefully controlled on Necromunda; regulated by the Imperial House and tithed to the Black Ships in accordance with the Emperor's laws. While the most powerful or dangerous psykers are contained and either disposed of immediately or shipped off-world to serve the Imperium, Lord Helmawr maintains a stock of gifted individuals for his own personal needs, and those of his favoured servants.

BELLADONNA, NOBLE BOUNTY HUNTRESS

As the ancient saying goes '*don't mess with a woman wronged*', and Belladonna has been oh so wronged! The noble bounty huntress is one of the seven daughters of Orlena Escher – matriarch of the Seven Spire Killer Cult – and once one of the most feared assassins in the Palatine Cluster. In a rare example of direct cooperation between a Clan House and a Noble House, Orlena compacted Belladonna to wed Tzakwon Ran Lo, heir to the Ran Lo Stratoplane Empire. Unusually for a marriage arranged solely for strategic gain, the two fell madly in love and everything went perfectly – that is, until the wedding day. In the midst of the betrothal banquet, with thousands of high-ranking guests in attendance, one of the wedding gifts began to growl. No sooner had Tzakwon looked within the ornate box than a starved Crotalid burst forth, tearing him apart in an explosion of gore. Anarchy erupted as the rabid beast ripped, snapped and clawed its way along the top table, until Belladonna leapt upon its back, brandishing in one hand a stiletto-heeled marriage shoe worth more than a House industrial helot would earn in a decade. Maintaining a curiously angelic visage, she drove the shoe's heel through one of the creature's eyes, impaling its brain and killing it in an instant. The struggle lasted mere seconds, but it cost the bride her left arm and leg, one eye, and left her lying in a pile of scattered food, broken furniture and mangled wedding guests.

Her House being expert in arcane medicae processes, Belladonna's injuries, which might otherwise have proved fatal, were quickly healed. She set out to exact her revenge within days, the scars around her new bionics still fresh, her wedding ribbons still stained with blood. Now she stalks the underhive as a Bounty Hunter for hire, seeking her husband's killers and the identity of the mysterious faction that sundered the alliance of Escher and Ran Lo before the ink was even dry on the marriage compact.

BELLADONNA, BOUNTY HUNTER

275 CREDITS

M	WS	BS	S	T	W	I	A	Ld	Cl	Wil	Int
6"	2+	5+	3	3	2	3+	2	7+	7+	6+	6+

Weapon	Rng S	Rng L	Acc S	Acc L	Str	AP	D	Am	Traits
Power axe	-	E	-	-	S+2	-2	1	-	Disarm, Melee, Power
Stiletto knife	-	E	-	-	-	-	-	-	Melee, Toxin
Fighting knife	-	E	-	-	S	-1	1	-	Backstab, Melee
Plasma pistol									
- low	6"	12"	+2	-	5	-1	2	5+	Scarce, Sidearm
- maximal	6"	12"	+1	-	7	-2	3	5+	Scarce, Sidearm, Unstable

SKILLS: Berserker, Combat Master, True Grit

WARGEAR: Light carapace armour

THE DESERTER, HUMAN BOUNTY HUNTER

No one knows the real name of the Deserter, only that by his tattoos he once served in the legendary Necromundan 8th. The crazy old soldier lives downhive in a booby-trapped warren, with every approach a deadly killing ground. Leaders often need to send at least a few Juves when contracting the Deserter, as he can be a little trigger happy when it comes to those who knock on his door. The skills he brings to a fight, however, are always worth it, and there are few individuals as talented when it comes to laying traps or setting ambushes.

Why the authorities tolerate the Deserter is a mystery to underhive gangs. Some believe he was a disgraced general that lost his entire regiment in some off-world war, and was given the choice of execution or exile to hive bottom. Others reckon he was a war hero, grievously wounded (as his skull plate seems to attest), who wandered down from the spire after losing his memory. Then there are those who say he is called the Deserter because that is just what he is, and Helmawr's cronies simply stopped trying to bring him in after their enforcers kept failing to come back. Whatever the truth, the Deserter is a cantankerous old fighter that gang fighters underestimate at their peril!

THE DESERTER, BOUNTY HUNTER

225 CREDITS

M	WS	BS	S	T	W	I	A	LD	CL	WIL	INT
4"	3+	4+	3	4	2	4+	2	7+	6+	7+	8+

Weapon	Rng S	Rng L	Acc S	Acc L	Str	AP	D	Am	Traits
Shotgun – solid	8"	16"	+1	-	4	-	2	4+	Knockback
Shotgun – scatter	4"	8"	+2	-	2	-	1	4+	Scattershot
Frag grenades	-	Sx3	-	-	3	-	1	4+	Blast (3"), Grenade, Knockback
Fighting knife	-	E	-	-	S	-1	1	-	Backstab, Melee

SKILLS: Medicae, Mentor, Overseer

WARGEAR: Armoured undersuit, flak armour

EYROS SLAGMYST, ENHANCED BOUNTY HUNTER

Eyros was once an underhive dome-rigger from Cogtown, one of the sweating, emaciated souls responsible for repairing the rusting pipe networks that fed the dismal settlement. When the Eye-Blight came to Cogtown, and its population began to die, Eyros and a group of dome-riggers set off into the underhive to find the scrap-tech to save their town. Deep down in the sump wells, close to hive bottom, the scavenging party found a vault of hidden treasures, among them a wondrous contraption that could extract life-giving water from almost anything. It was Eyros who donned the strange archaeo-rig, its syringes and bone-flutes burrowing into his flesh until all his organs pulsed in time with the machine. Unfortunately for Eyros, though it gave him strength and life, it also gave him a burning thirst.

As it turned out, while water can be found in many things, few things in Necromunda have quite as much as humans. After Eyros had drained his companions, he returned to Cogtown and left only dust and scrap in his wake. He soon discovered that the potent fluids concocted in the harness could also be dispensed to his allies, and it was not long before Eyros began selling his services and 'water' to gangs in exchange for fresh subjects to drink from. These days it is hard to tell how much of Eyros is left under the archaeo-cybernetics that have taken root within him, his features hidden under writhing wires and pitted armour. There is also no telling what Eyros will become once the archaeotech is done with him.

EYROS SLAGMYST, BOUNTY HUNTER — 270 CREDITS

M	WS	BS	S	T	W	I	A	Ld	Cl	Wil	Int
4"	3+	4+	3	4	2	5+	1	5+	7+	5+	5+

Weapon	Rng S	Rng L	Acc S	Acc L	Str	AP	D	Am	Traits
Laspistol	8"	12"	+1	-	3	-	1	2+	Plentiful, Sidearm
Frag grenades	-	Sx3	-	-	3	-	1	4+	Blast (3"), Grenade, Knockback
Fighting knife	-	E	-	-	S	-1	1	-	Backstab, Melee

SKILLS: Iron Jaw, Nerves of Steel, True Grit

WARGEAR: Armoured undersuit, bio-booster, furnace plates, medicae kit, photo-goggles

GOR HALF-HORN, BOUNTY HUNTER

235 CREDITS

M	WS	BS	S	T	W	I	A		LD	CL	WIL	INT
4"	3+	4+	4	4	2	4+	1		5+	6+	6+	6+

Weapon	Rng S	Rng L	Acc S	Acc L	Str	AP	D	Am	Traits
Chainsword	-	E	-	+1	S	-1	1	-	Melee, Parry, Rending
Plasma pistol (low)	6"	12"	+2	-	5	-1	2	5+	Scarce, Sidearm
Plasma pistol (max)	6"	12"	+1	-	7	-2	3	5+	Scarce, Sidearm, Unstable
Shotgun (solid)	8"	16"	+1	-	4	-	2	4+	Knockback
Shotgun (scatter)	4"	8"	+2	-	2	-	1	4+	Scattershot

SKILLS: Berserker, Bull Charge, Fearsome

WARGEAR: Flak armour

GRENDL GRENDLSEN, SQUAT BOUNTY HUNTER

As a banner-jarl in the famed Vega Rams mercenary company, Grendl came to Necromunda with the Rogue Trader Lord Constant Gerrit of the Arcadius dynasty's guard of honour. But while his liege was entertained in the undreamed-of luxury of Lord Helmawr's spire-palace, the Abhuman members of his household, including the entire complement of the Vega Rams, were required to remain in the Stranger's Tower, as they were forbidden to set foot in the hive proper. In some ways, it is fortunate for Grendl that he was not present when the wing of the Helmawr Palace-spire in which Constant Gerrit was being housed was destroyed by a low-yield atomic charge planted by a rival House; yet in others it was unfortunate, for in the subsequent household purge, Grendl was forced to flee, seeking sanctuary in the anonymous squalor of the underhive.

Despite the dire circumstances of his coming to Hive Primus, Grendl Grendlsen quickly established a new life, finding gainful employ as a bodyguard to various underhive figures. At length, he earned the right to practice as a sanctioned Bounty Hunter, and now serves any master who will pay his fee. Grendl is famed for protecting his charges from their rivals and subsequently claiming the bounty on the would-be assassins' heads, and so far there has been no shortage of foolhardy rivals eager to test his skills, and his infamous hammer.

GRENDL GRENDLSEN, BOUNTY HUNTER

280 CREDITS

M	WS	BS	S	T	W	I	A	Ld	Cl	Wil	Int
3"	3+	4+	3	4	3	5+	1	5+	7+	5+	5+

Weapon	Rng S	Rng L	Acc S	Acc L	Str	AP	D	Am	Traits
Boltgun	12"	24"	+1	-	4	-1	2	6+	Rapid Fire (1)
Power hammer	-	E	-	-	S+1	-1	2	-	Melee, Power
Frag grenades	-	Sx3	-	-	3	-	1	4+	Blast (3"), Grenade, Knockback

SKILLS: Combat Master, Iron Jaw, Nerves of Steel
WARGEAR: Armoured undersuit, flak armour

GRUB TARGESON (AKA LUMPY NOX) – HIVE SCUM

Not so long ago, Grub was an upstanding member of the Merchant Guild in Hive Primus. Every day, thousands of creds ran through his thick fingers and the fates of thousands of workers rested on his every nod or sneer. Then, one day, he woke up to find an odd lump growing out of his shoulder. At first Grub paid it no mind, as minor mutations and strange diseases are a common sight throughout the hive, and he simply asked his stitch-master to loosen the seams on his coats. As the cycles ground by, the lump grew, with Grub finding it harder and harder to hide his growing deformity. Then one day it spoke to him – which was when Grub fled to the underhive.

Now Grub wanders the underhive, whispering conversations with his hump and hiring himself out to gangs that need extra firepower. Most pass off his ramblings as the results of one too many bottles of Second Best, though some swear they have heard the hump talking back to Grub. Perhaps most disturbing of all is that Grub seems to know things he shouldn't – such as where stashes are hidden or when a hive quake might be coming – each time stroking his hump affectionately when one of his predictions comes true…

GRUB TARGESON, HIVE SCUM

105 CREDITS

M	WS	BS	S	T	W	I	A	Ld	Cl	Wil	Int
4"	4+	3+	3	3	1	4+	1	8+	8+	8+	6+

Weapon	Rng S	Rng L	Acc S	Acc L	Str	AP	D	Am	Traits
Fighting knife	-	E	-	-	S	-1	1	-	Backstab, Melee
Shotgun									
- scatter	4"	8"	+2	-	2	-	1	4+	Scattershot
- executioner	4"	16"	-1	+1	4	-2	2	6+	Knockback, Limited
Frag grenades	-	Sx3	-	-	3	-	1	4+	Blast (3"), Grenade, Knockback

SKILLS: Backstab, Evade, Infiltrate

WARGEAR: Flak armour

KRIA 'THE HUNTRESS' KYTORO, HOUSE ESCHER DEATH-MAIDEN BOUNTY HUNTER

Kria Kytoro died with a sneer on her lips and her blade buried in her rival's throat. Single-minded in her pursuit of her enemies, Kria earned the moniker of 'Huntress' because none prey-marked by her crew, the Bittersweet Blades, ever escaped for long. When Kria tangled with Gorgon, boss of the Irontree Lords, she met her match in ferocity and cunning, the Goliath leader emptying his shotgun into Kria's chest even as her knife opened up his throat. Kria's story might have ended there, had the alchymyst fleshteks of House Escher not already had their eye on her. Hauling her body from the Sump, the fleshteks began the process to turn Kria into a death-maiden, a resurrected warrior of House Escher. Kria proved an excellent subject, and within the cycle, she was hauling herself from an amniotic tank, her veins pulsing with chems.

Death-maidens are assassins, fixers and enforcers for the House – bringing the will of the matriarchy into the depths of the underhive. Brought back from the edge of oblivion by alchemical means; their blood is transfused with a cocktail of chems and their minds stripped of whatever shreds of humanity they once had. Usually, death-maidens run alone, joining Escher crews to enforce the interests of the House, though it is not unheard of for entire gangs of death-maidens to gather when the matriarch council calls – such as in the War for Hive Mortis.

For Kria, the mantle of death-maiden rests well upon her shoulders, and dying and coming back from the beyond has done little to diminish her skills as a tracker and hunter. Her toxic blood also means that she can always wet her weapons with poison before the kill, and she savours the look in her prey's eyes as she draws a knife across her own flesh.

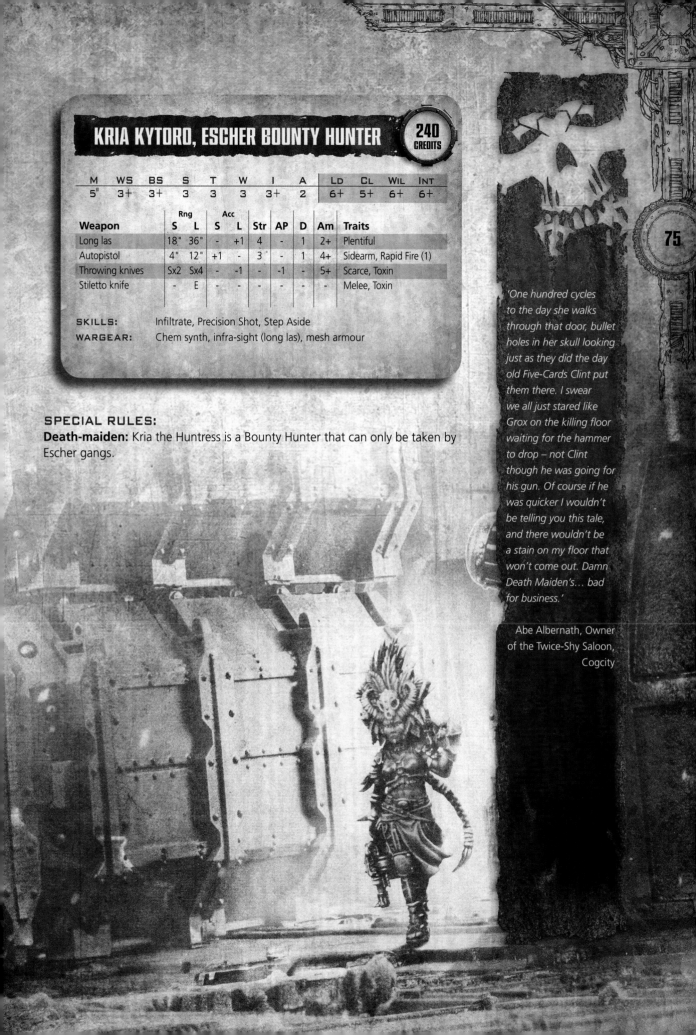

KRIA KYTORO, ESCHER BOUNTY HUNTER

240 CREDITS

M	WS	BS	S	T	W	I	A	Ld	Cl	Wil	Int
5"	3+	3+	3	3	3	3+	2	6+	5+	6+	6+

Weapon	Rng S	Rng L	Acc S	Acc L	Str	AP	D	Am	Traits
Long las	18"	36"	-	+1	4	-	1	2+	Plentiful
Autopistol	4"	12"	+1	-	3	-	1	4+	Sidearm, Rapid Fire (1)
Throwing knives	Sx2	Sx4	-	-1	-	-1	-	5+	Scarce, Toxin
Stiletto knife	-	E	-	-	-	-	-	-	Melee, Toxin

SKILLS: Infiltrate, Precision Shot, Step Aside

WARGEAR: Chem synth, infra-sight (long las), mesh armour

SPECIAL RULES:

Death-maiden: Kria the Huntress is a Bounty Hunter that can only be taken by Escher gangs.

'One hundred cycles to the day she walks through that door, bullet holes in her skull looking just as they did the day old Five-Cards Clint put them there. I swear we all just stared like Grox on the killing floor waiting for the hammer to drop – not Clint though he was going for his gun. Of course if he was quicker I wouldn't be telling you this tale, and there wouldn't be a stain on my floor that won't come out. Damn Death Maiden's... bad for business.'

Abe Albernath, Owner of the Twice-Shy Saloon, Cogcity

KROTOS HARK, BOUNTY HUNTER

220 CREDITS

M	WS	BS	S	T	W	I	A	Ld	Cl	Wil	Int
4"	3+	4+	3	4	2	4+	2	7+	4+	7+	4+

Weapon	Rng S	Rng L	Acc S	Acc L	Str	AP	D	Am	Traits
Stub cannon	9"	18"	-	-	5	-	1	3+	Knockback
Fighting knife	-	E	-	-	S	-1	1	-	Backstab, Melee

SKILLS: Headbutt, Inspirational, Munitioneer

WARGEAR: Armoured undersuit, furnace plates

KROTOS HARK, GOLIATH BOUNTY HUNTER

Not all Goliaths emerge from the flesh vats disciplined and subservient. Once in a thousand cycles, something goes awry and an aberration is born. Usually these failed gestations are quickly purged, but sometimes the mutation is more subtle. Krotos Hark was born with that most dangerous of gifts; intelligence. He was clever enough to hide his keen mind, and managed to survive long enough to make his way into one of the House gangs. Rather than fight his way up to leadership, something he could certainly have done, he set his sights on a grander destiny.

Hark is a skilled armourer, and valued among gangs for his ability to improve the weapons and gear of those willing to pay. His own furnace plate armour has been hardened against all manner of weapons, while his mask not only hides his identity from his former masters, but can turn aside rounds. Though Hark remains tight-lipped about his ultimate ambitions, it has not gone unnoticed that he seems to be gathering allies and contacts every time he works a contract or fills a bounty. He also seems to take a special interest in jobs that oppose House Goliath. All of this makes some speculate that perhaps Hark is looking to make a permanent change of management among his old bosses.

MAD DOG MONO – HIVE SCUM

Mono works the great Ash Gates of Port Mad Dog when he is not hiring out his services as a mercenary to gangs, Ash Wasters and outlaws alike. Born into the Longshore clans, he grew up on the edges of the Palatine Cluster, the great hives visible only as shadows against the toxic horizon, their spires taunting him with the promise of safety and wealth. Life for a Longshore clanner is usually short and brutal – if the poisonous winds don't get them, then a faulty cargo lifter, angry Ash Waster or wandering wasteland creature probably will. Mono's fate was changed, however, when a scavvy trader sold him a strange one-eyed hood. It turned out to be an ancient strato-pilot helmet, and as Mono discovered, its oculus-augur gave him a unique view of the world, and amazing reactions as a result.

After carving up a bar full of drunken mag-line dusters with his grab-hook, Mono realised that he had a talent for mayhem and put the word out he was looking for 'extra work'. It wasn't long before Mono had made a name for himself bringing down Three-toes Jack during the Rustfalls uprising and running with the Sump City Sirens during their takeover of the Delta Zone Dust Wells. Despite his success, Mono always returns to Port Mad Dog, for as the Longshore clanners always say – 'blood is thicker than ash'.

MAD DOG MONO, HIVE SCUM — 90 CREDITS

M	WS	BS	S	T	W	I	A	Ld	Cl	Wil	Int
5"	3+	4+	3	3	1	3+	1	8+	7+	8+	8+

Weapon	Rng S	Rng L	Acc S	Acc L	Str	AP	D	Am	Traits
Stub gun	6"	12"	+2	-	3	-	1	4+	Plentiful, Sidearm
Grab hook	E	2"	-	-	S	-	1	-	Disarm, Melee, Versatile

SKILLS: Dodge, Escape Artist

WARGEAR: Boiler plate armour (which works just like Goliath furnace plate armour but is made from scraps salvaged from derelict Ash Wastes transports), respirator

SLATE MERDENA, ORLOCK ROAD BOSS BOUNTY HUNTER

The Sump Dogs are one of the hardest gangs to ever ride the ash roads of the Spider Points, and their success can be attributed to one man: Slate Merdena. As a juve out of Sumptown, Slate built his first runner out of scrap, and took down his first Waster caravan before he could shave. It wasn't long before he had his own crew, and not long after that a gang of riders he called the Sump Dogs, in memory of his hometown. Soon, the Sump Dogs boasted gangs from one end of the Palatine Cluster to the other and Slate was infamous for giving beaten Orlock leaders a choice between donning his colours or taking a short ride on the end of chain behind his war-rig! Despite his successes, when the masters of House Orlock called Slate to court for his well-earned place among them, he refused – unwilling to give up the road. Not wanting to lose such a talented fighter, or perhaps concerned what Slate might do if they trifled with him, they instead made him a Road Boss – a master of multiple gangs and an agent for the House masters themselves.

Slate controls a dozen Hive Primus Ash Gates in the name of House Orlock, and a dozen more have made deals with his fighters for protection. Over the years countless other gangs have tried to take him out, and Slate has earned a reputation for being nigh unkillable – having survived bullets to the chest, blades between his shoulders and even being hurled under the wheels of his own rig. Though time has taken its toll on Slate, evidenced by the dust visor he wears to hide his ash-burned eyes, he still radiates power. Often the mere sight of Slate and his faithful Cyber-mastiff, Macula, are enough to send his enemies running – lest they end their days as a mile marker on the Spider Points like so many before them.

SLATE MERDENA, ORLOCK BOUNTY HUNTER

360 CREDITS

M	WS	BS	S	T	W	I	A	Ld	Cl	Wil	Int
5"	2+	3+	3	4	3	3+	3	4+	5+	4+	5+

Weapon	Rng S	Rng L	Acc S	Acc L	Str	AP	D	Am	Traits
Custom Plasma pistol									
- low	12"	24"	+2	-	5	-1	2	5+	Scarce, Sidearm
- maximal	12"	24"	+1	-	7	-2	3	5+	Scarce, Sidearm, Unstable
Power hammer	-	E	-	-	S+1	-1	2	-	Melee, Power

SKILLS: Fearsome, Iron Will, Nerves of Steel

WARGEAR: Cyber-mastiff, frag grenades, mesh armour, photo-goggles

SPECIAL RULES

Orlock Road Boss: Slate Merdena is a Bounty Hunter that can only be taken by Orlock gangs.

MACULA, CYBER-MASTIFF

– CREDITS

M	WS	BS	S	T	W	I	A	Ld	Cl	Wil	Int
5"	3+	-	3	3	2	4+	2	7+	6+	8+	9+

Weapon	Rng S	Rng L	Acc S	Acc L	Str	AP	D	Am	Traits
Savage bite	-	E	-	-	S	-2	1	-	Disarm, Melee

SKILLS: Combat Master

SPECIAL RULES: Loyal Protector, Watchdog

'Slate doesn't win fights, he just allows you to lose.'

Sump Dogs saying

YAR UMBRA, VOID-BORN BOUNTY HUNTER

Vast quantities of off-world trade comes to Necromunda via the Eye of Selene. Carrying these cargoes are all manner of ships, their crews often made up of void-born spacers who spend their lives traversing the inky galactic wilds. Yar Umbra came to Hive Primus on the chartist vessel the *Halcyon Dawn*. Unfortunately for Yar, when his ship left he was not on it, for he was intentionally marooned by the deck master for some unknown infraction, which, some say, was centred around what it is that he hides beneath his hood.

Embittered by his abandonment, Yar yearns to return to the stars, and has turned his talents to claiming bounties, in the hopes of one day obtaining passage on a vessel and hunting down the *Halcyon Dawn*. In the interim, Yar has found that though he despises his planet-bound existence, he is very much at home in the confined tunnels of Necromunda. The stinking depths of a hive are much the same as those of a void ship (if even a bit more forgiving), and equipped with enviro-filters and gas-plugs, Yar is well-protected from local hazards. Darkness is also an environment Yar knows well, and with his custom maw-pattern long las even a flicker of movement is enough for the void-born sniper to bring down his prey.

YAR UMBRA, BOUNTY HUNTER

230 CREDITS

M	WS	BS	S	T	W	I	A	Ld	Cl	Wil	Int
4"	4+	2+	3	4	2	3+	1	7+	5+	7+	7+

Weapon	Rng S	Rng L	Acc S	Acc L	Str	AP	D	Am	Traits
Long las	18"	36"	-	+1	4	-	1	2+	Plentiful
Fighting knife	-	E	-	-	S	-1	1	-	Backstab, Melee

SKILLS: Infiltrate, Marksman, Overwatch

WARGEAR: Flak armour, infra-sight, photo-goggles, respirator

YOLANDA SKORN, BOUNTY HUNTER

There is usually little mercy for gangers who challenge their leaders and fail, and most end their days rotting at the bottom of the Sump. Sometimes, though, a rival is so impressive, simple execution seems like a waste. This was the case for the Escher Bounty Hunter Yolanda Skorn. The leader of her former gang, the Bloodmaidens, looked into her crazed eyes, even as she grinned through sheets of blood from her freshly carved exile scars and decided nothing so cruel and beautiful could be taken from the world.

Skorn's missing hand, lost in the duel, was replaced with a whirring cybernetic, and she adopted a veil to hide her facial scars (mostly so they didn't unsettle her allies), before setting off on a journey of murder and mayhem. As anyone who has met her will attest, Skorn is quite insane. She constantly talks to her weapons, doors, the walls and anything else that crosses her path. She also enjoys close-in kills, sometimes pulling aside her veil so her enemies can see her scars 'smile' before they die. Understandably, Yolanda Skorn's reputation precedes her most places she goes, and the mere sight of her can send some enemies running. It also means she seldom stays with the one employer for long, as there is only so many times a gang leader can wake up with Skorn's staring eyes an inch from their face before deciding that enough is enough.

YOLANDA SKORN, BOUNTY HUNTER — 230 CREDITS

M	WS	BS	S	T	W	I	A	Ld	Cl	Wil	Int
5"	3+	3+	3	3	2	3+	2	7+	5+	6+	6+

Weapon	Rng S	Rng L	Acc S	Acc L	Str	AP	D	Am	Traits
Stiletto knife	-	E	-	-	-	-	-	-	Melee, Toxin
Stub gun	6"	12"	+2	-	3	-	1	4+	Plentiful, Sidearm
Frag grenades	-	Sx3	-	-	3	-	1	4+	Blast (3"), Grenade, Knockback

SKILLS: Counter-attack, Fearsome, Parry
WARGEAR: Flak armour, photo-goggles, respirator

HANGERS-ON AND BRUTES

Once a gang establishes itself, its hideout can become as well known as any other local landmark. Some gangs' hideouts become centres of activity, with loyal hivers granted the freedom to come and go as they please, while others are more like fortresses. In either case, they are sought-after destinations for merchants and tradesmen seeking a reliable base of operations and offering their services to the gang.

Hangers-on are primarily used in Campaign play, although some will prove particularly useful in Skirmish games. Brutes are purchased specifically to add some extra muscle and prowess on the battlefield and can be fielded alongside the rest of the gang normally. In the Update Roster step of the post-battle sequence, players can recruit Hangers-on and Brutes. These are purchased with credits from the gang's Stash in the same way as new fighters. A Fighter card is filled out for them and they are added to the gang roster. Most Hangers-on and Brutes have various options for their equipment – these must be decided when they are recruited.

The maximum number of Hangers-on and Brutes a gang can have is limited by their Reputation, as shown by the table below. If a gang's Reputation drops to the point they do not have enough for their Hangers-on or Brutes, they must remove one or more of them from their roster until they are back within their limit. Also, note that there is a limit on each type of Hanger-on and Brute – a gang can have up to two Rogue Docs, but only one Dome Runner, for example. Hangers-on and Brutes do not count towards the number of fighters in the gang; for example, they are not counted when determining how many Gangers the gang must contain.

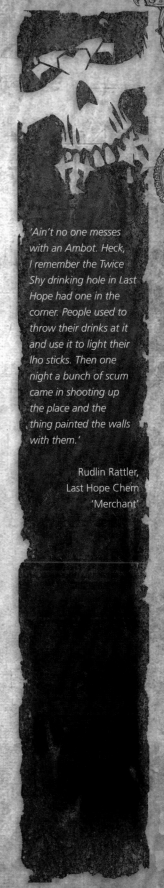

'Ain't no one messes with an Ambot. Heck, I remember the Twice Shy drinking hole in Last Hope had one in the corner. People used to throw their drinks at it and use it to light their lho sticks. Then one night a bunch of scum came in shooting up the place and the thing painted the walls with them.'

Rudlin Rattler,
Last Hope Chem
'Merchant'

Reputation	Maximum Hangers-on
Less than 5	1
5-9	2
10-14	3
15-19	4
20-24	5
Each additional 5	+1

Each of the types of Hangers-on gives a gang a special rule, but they do not normally take part in battles. However, whenever a battle happens on the gang's turf (i.e., they have the Home Turf Advantage in a scenario), roll a D6 for each of their Hangers-on before choosing a crew. On a result of 1, 2 or 3, the Hanger-on is unfortunate enough to be around when the fighting starts, and must be included as a part of the crew. Hangers-on cannot gain Experience or Advancements; if they suffer a Lasting Injury that would make a change to their Fighter card, they decide that the hideout is no longer safe and move on – they are removed from the gang roster. They cannot be given any equipment other than what is listed.

Brutes, however, are purchased with the express intention that they be fielded in battle and are treated like any other fighter when selecting a crew. Unlike other Hangers-on, Brutes will gain Experience and Advancements in the same manner as a Specialist Ganger, and their skill set access is detailed below. Unlike other Hangers-on, Brutes will not leave the gang should they suffer a Lasting Injury that makes a change to their Fighter card. They also cannot be given any equipment other than what is listed.

Both Hangers-on and Brutes can be taken Captive, in which case the gang can attempt to rescue them and the capturing gang may sell them as if they were a normal fighter.

	Agility	Brawn	Combat	Cunning	Ferocity	Leadership	Shooting	Savant
Luther Pattern Excavation Automata	-	Secondary	Secondary	-	Primary	-	-	-
'Jotunn' Servitor Ogryn	-	Primary	Secondary	-	Secondary	-	-	-
Stig-shambler	-	Primary	Secondary	Secondary	-	-	-	Primary
Delaque Spyker	Secondary	-	-	Secondary	-	-	-	Primary
Escher Khimerix	Secondary	-	Secondary	-	Primary	-	-	-
Goliath 'Zerker	-	Primary	Secondary	-	Secondary	-	-	-
Orlock 'Lugger'	-	Secondary	Secondary	-	-	-	Primary	-
Van Saar 'Arachni-rig'	-	Secondary	-	-	Secondary	-	Primary	-

HANGERS-ON

0-2 ROGUE DOCS ....50 CREDITS

Medical expertise is much sought-after in the underhive, and most of those who have such training sell their services at a not insignificant price. However, should tragedy befall one of these 'docs' – perhaps an influential gang leader dies under their scalpel, or they are blamed for an outbreak of sickness – they will throw in their lot with a friendly gang, trading their expertise for protection.

If a gang has a Rogue Doc, it can make an additional Medical Escort action in the post-battle sequence (see page 92 in the *Necromunda Rulebook*) in addition to any other actions made by the gang's Leader or Champions. This visit does not cost any credits – however, a result of 6 on the table is treated as Stabilised rather than a Full Recovery, thanks to the Doc's comparatively limited supplies and the lack of proper medical technology. If a gang has more than one Rogue Doc, it can make this additional action once for each of them.

M	WS	BS	S	T	W	I	A	Ld	Cl	Wil	Int
5"	5+	5+	2	3	1	4+	1	9+	8+	7+	5+

EQUIPMENT
Laspistol or stub gun; medicae kit

SKILLS
Medicae

0-3 AMMO-JACKS ....50 CREDITS

As gangs become more experienced, they discover the importance of regular weapon checks. Running out of ammunition or suffering a gun jam in the middle of a firefight is just not acceptable for a gang that wishes to be taken seriously. As such, many take on full-time armourers, setting up a workshop within their hideout to ensure that such mishaps are far less likely.

If a gang has an Ammo-jack, its weapons are regularly serviced and their ammo stocks are carefully maintained. As such, fighters from the gang can re-roll any failed Ammo checks that roll a natural 1. The Ammo-jack does not have to take part in the battle for the gang to receive this bonus, but if they are not available for the battle – for example, if they are In Recovery or have been Captured, the bonus does not apply.

If a gang has more than one Ammo-jack, the bonus increases. A gang with two Ammo-jacks can re-roll failed Ammo checks that roll a natural 1 or 2. A gang with three can re-roll failed Ammo checks that roll a natural 1, 2 or 3.

M	WS	BS	S	T	W	I	A	Ld	Cl	Wil	Int
5"	4+	3+	3	3	1	5+	1	9+	7+	6+	7+

EQUIPMENT
Boltgun or combat shotgun with salvo and shredder ammo; power hammer or power sword; mesh armour

SKILLS
Munitioneer

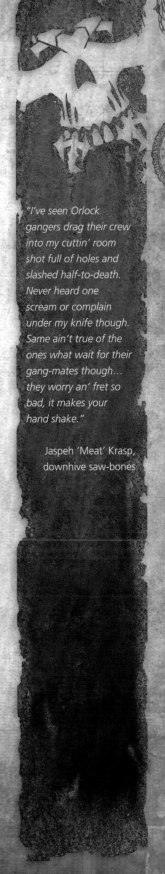

"I've seen Orlock gangers drag their crew into my cuttin' room shot full of holes and slashed half-to-death. Never heard one scream or complain under my knife though. Same ain't true of the ones what wait for their gang-mates though… they worry an' fret so bad, it makes your hand shake."

Jaspeh 'Meat' Krasp, downhive saw-bones

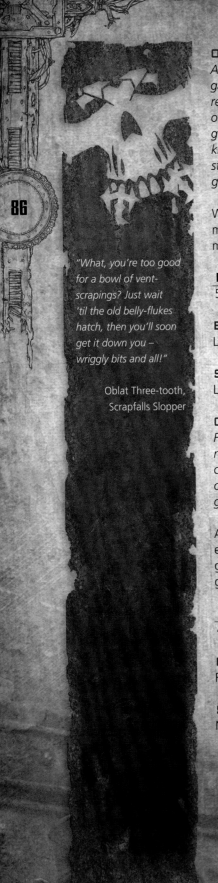

0-1 DOME RUNNER ....20 CREDITS

A gang's Turf is its primary source of income, but as it expands outwards, the gangers might find themselves in areas they've never even visited. Local guides, referred to as 'Dome Runners', are a regular sight among gangs wishing to root out this new turf's hidden treasures. Runners come from a variety of backgrounds, generally unfortunate, but they all have one thing in common: an exhaustive knowledge of the local area and a distinct lack of other marketable skills. From stick-thin waifs to gnarled ex-gangers, these vagabonds gladly settle down with a gang in exchange for reliable shelter.

Whenever a fighter from a gang with a Dome Runner opens a loot casket, they may choose to re-roll the D6 to determine what the contents are. However, they must accept the result of the re-roll, even if it is worse.

M	WS	BS	S	T	W	I	A	Ld	Cl	Wil	Int
5"	5+	5+	3	3	1	3+	1	10+	9+	7+	8+

EQUIPMENT
Laspistol or stub gun; fighting knife or axe

SKILLS
Lie Low

"What, you're too good for a bowl of vent-scrapings? Just wait 'til the old belly-flukes hatch, then you'll soon get it down you – wriggly bits and all!"

Oblat Three-tooth, Scrapfalls Slopper

0-1 SLOPPER ....20 CREDITS

Food in the underhive rarely holds any joy. Most meals consist of corpse-starch or nutri-slime, supplemented with synth-fats and vitamin shots. As such, anyone who can produce 'real' food from the local flora and fauna can expect a steady stream of credits. They are usually keen to set up a kitchen in a gang's headquarters; they get somewhere secure to store their wares, and the gang gets its share of leftovers.

At the end of the Spend Experience step of the pre-battle sequence, roll a D6 for each of the gang's fighters that is In Recovery. On a roll of 6, a constant supply of good food has helped them recover more quickly – their In Recovery box on the gang roster is cleared, and are now available for this battle.

M	WS	BS	S	T	W	I	A	Ld	Cl	Wil	Int
4"	4+	4+	2	3	1	3+	1	9+	9+	5+	7+

EQUIPMENT
Fighting knife

SKILLS
None

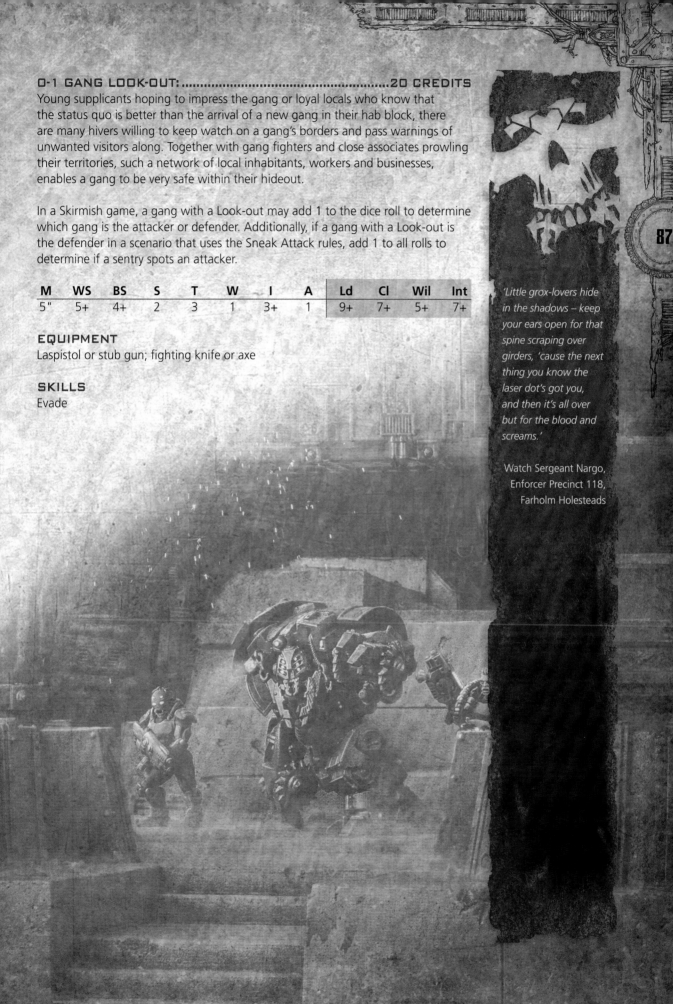

0-1 GANG LOOK-OUT: ....20 CREDITS

Young supplicants hoping to impress the gang or loyal locals who know that the status quo is better than the arrival of a new gang in their hab block, there are many hivers willing to keep watch on a gang's borders and pass warnings of unwanted visitors along. Together with gang fighters and close associates prowling their territories, such a network of local inhabitants, workers and businesses, enables a gang to be very safe within their hideout.

In a Skirmish game, a gang with a Look-out may add 1 to the dice roll to determine which gang is the attacker or defender. Additionally, if a gang with a Look-out is the defender in a scenario that uses the Sneak Attack rules, add 1 to all rolls to determine if a sentry spots an attacker.

M	WS	BS	S	T	W	I	A	Ld	Cl	Wil	Int
5"	5+	4+	2	3	1	3+	1	9+	7+	5+	7+

EQUIPMENT
Laspistol or stub gun; fighting knife or axe

SKILLS
Evade

'Little grox-lovers hide in the shadows – keep your ears open for that spine scraping over girders, 'cause the next thing you know the laser dot's got you, and then it's all over but for the blood and screams.'

Watch Sergeant Nargo, Enforcer Precinct 118, Farholm Holesteads

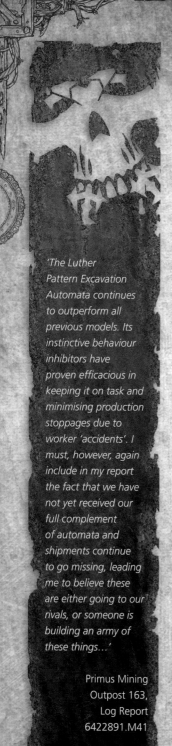

BRUTES
0-2 LUTHER PATTERN EXCAVATION AUTOMATA
('AMBOT') .... 215 CREDITS

The Luther pattern Excavation Automata is a heavy construct built in imitation of the Ambull, a huge, roughly humanoid xenos creature common to hot, arid worlds. Thought to have evolved in the endless deserts of Luther McIntyre IX in the Segmentum Solar, the Ambull is now common across the Imperium, Humanity having attempted to domesticate the brutes to make use of their traits. Ambulls are natural tunnellers, their powerful limbs ending in diamond-hard claws that enable them to dig through soft rock at a surprising speed. Their eyes see into the infrared spectrum, making impeccable use of even the faintest levels of light, and they are even able to detect heat signatures as a visual stimulus.

The transport and trade in Ambulls is extremely heavily controlled throughout the Imperium, due to how dangerous they are as hunters and how unsuitable to domestication they have proven, escaping from any form of captivity and wreaking havoc upon human populations in mining colonies the galaxy over.

The greatest successes in domesticating the Ambull lie in using the creatures as the organic component of a heavy mining construct. Specially crafted instrumentalities are fused with the brain and nervous system of the Ambull, in a process perfected by the Adeptus Mechanicus, to circumvent the most ancient of laws proscribing the 'machina malifica', the dreaded 'machine that thinks'. When the creature awakens in its new robotic shell, it retains the natural tunnelling instinct it had when it was flesh, whilst its aggression and hunting impulses are suppressed by cranial governors. Consequently, Luther pattern Excavation Automata, or 'Ambots', as they are commonly called in the underhive vernacular, are not uncommon on Necromunda, where they are utilised for slag mining and ash excavation. A common danger of using such constructs, however, is that there is always an underhive gang waiting for the opportunity to liberate such a prized commodity, and utilise it as a weapon against their rivals!

M	WS	BS	S	T	W	I	A	Ld	Cl	Wil	Int
4"	3+	5+	5	5	3	5+	2	8+	6+	8+	9+

Weapon	Rng S	Rng L	Acc S	Acc L	S	AP	D	Am	Traits
Tunnelling claw									
- melee	-	E	-	-	S	-1	2	-	Melee
- ranged	4"	8"	-	-	6	-2	2	5+	Melta, Scarce, Sidearm
Grav-fist									
- melee	-	E	-	-	S	-1	2	-	Melee, Pulverise
- ranged	6"	12"	+1	-	*	-1	2	5+	Blast (3"), Graviton Pulse, Concussion

WEAPONS
An Ambot is armed with two tunnelling claws.

OPTIONS
• An Ambot may replace one of its tunnelling claws with a grav-fist...... +70 credits

SPECIAL RULES

Infiltrate: If this fighter should be set up at the start of the battle, they are instead placed to one side. Then, immediately before the first round, their controlling player sets them up anywhere on the battlefield that is not visible to any enemy fighters, and not within 6" of any of them. If both players have fighters with this skill, take turns to set one up, starting with the winner of a roll-off.

Cranial Governors: In normal circumstances, an Ambot's behaviour will be heavily governed to protect other workers from the aggressive instincts of the Ambull. Gangers, however, have no such safety concerns and will frequently switch off the inhibitors on an Ambot in their possession. When an Ambot is operating in Safe Mode it follows the rules and profile described previously. Should the controlling player wish, Safe Mode can be switched off at the beginning of any round. Whilst Safe Mode is off, the Ambot gains the Berserker (Ferocity) skill and its Attacks characteristic becomes D3+1. However, when Standing and Engaged, the Ambot must divide its attacks amongst all models it is in base-to-base contact with, including friendly fighters. Once Safe Mode is off, it cannot be reinitiated until the Wrap Up.

Mechanical Construction: An Ambot is equipped with light carapace armour.

Excavation Automata: If the gang that owns the Ambot also controls a Mine Workings territory, roll an additional D6 to generate income to represent the Ambot being put to work.

Valuable: Should an Ambot be Captured by a rival gang and not be rescued, the gang holding it Captive may choose to either sell it to the Guilders as a normal Captive, or to keep it and add it to their gang roster for free, assuming they have sufficient Reputation to take on an extra Hanger-on.

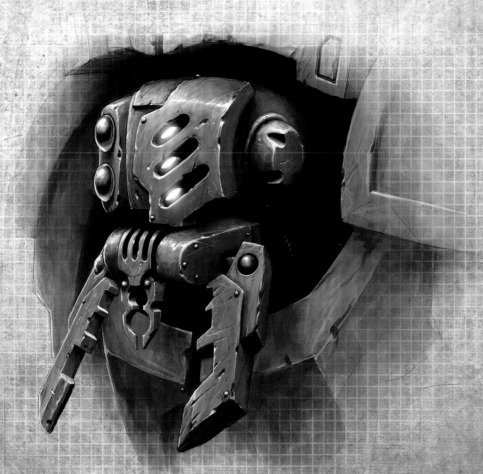

SCRAP-HACKED 'AMBOT'
HOUSE ORLOCK

0-2 'JOTUNN' H-GRADE SERVITOR OGRYN: .... 210 CREDITS

Homo sapiens gigantus, commonly called 'Ogryns', are one of the most frequently seen strains of abhuman within the Imperium. Their origin is believed to be a chain of high gravity prison worlds, populated by Mankind many millennia ago and lost during the Age of Strife. In isolation from Terra, the humans stranded upon these worlds bred and adapted to their hostile environments, becoming progressively larger and hardier with each passing generation. Unfortunately, intelligence, probably not that prominent a trait amongst the denizens of these prison worlds to begin with, deteriorated over the generations, so that by the time the Ogryn had become a distinct and stable sub-species of humanity, it was hopelessly dull and unintelligent.

Ogryns are incredibly strong, durable, and remarkably loyal, traits which make up for their lack of intellect in their usefulness to the Imperium. They are slow to learn, but once a lesson has been learned, it stays in their simple minds forever. These factors make Ogryns the ideal soldier for the Astra Militarum and their presence is prized amongst many regiments the galaxy over, where they are often employed as elite shock troops. They are equally well-suited to menial work, their strength and endurance enabling them to match the workload of several baseline humans in any given hard labour role, and even more when cybernetic enhancements are added into the equation.

M	WS	BS	S	T	W	I	A	Ld	Cl	Wil	Int
5"	4+	5+	5	5	3	4+	2	7+	6+	8+	9+

Weapon	Rng S	Rng L	Acc S	Acc L	S	AP	D	Am	Traits
Augmetic fist	-	E	-	-	S+1	-1	2	-	Melee, Knockback
Arc welder	-	E	-	-	S+2	-3	3	-	Melee, Blaze

WEAPONS
A 'Jotunn' H-Grade Servitor-Ogryn is armed with two augmetic fists.

OPTIONS
- A Servitor-Ogryn may replace one of its augmetic fists with an arc welder... +70 credits
- A Servitor-Ogryn may be upgraded with furnace plate armour............ +15 credits

SPECIAL RULES

Headbutt: If this fighter is Engaged, they can make the following action:

Headbutt (Basic) – Pick an Engaged enemy fighter and roll two D6. If either result is equal to or higher than their Toughness, they suffer a hit with a Strength equal to this fighter's Strength +2, resolved as Damage 2. However, if both dice score lower than the enemy fighter's Toughness, this fighter instead suffers a hit equal to their own Strength.

Loyal: Ogryns are very loyal creatures and form strong bonds with those that they live and fight with. Whenever a friendly fighter making a close combat attack claims an assist from this fighter, this fighter adds 2 to the result of any hit rolls, rather than the usual 1.

Slow-witted: Ogryns are not especially bright or quick on the uptake. This fighter may never be activated as part of a group activation.

T.H.R.U.G. 12 'SPARKY'
DAEYGLOW DRAGONS
HOUSE VAN SAAR

0-1 CAWDOR STIG-SHAMBLER .... 240 CREDITS

The preachers and rabble-rousers of the devout of House Cawdor have little tolerance for the mutant and the abhuman. Such deformities of the body are clear evidence, so their leaders tell them, of the corruption that lurks within the soul. How can anyone who lives their life in loyalty to the Emperor, anyone who dedicates their every action to His glory, their every moment of toil to the betterment of His Imperium, ever become so corrupt and debased of form? Physical abnormalities are clear evidence, then, that those afflicted have turned their gaze away from His light and shunned Him as their one true master, and so the devout of House Cawdor will hunt them down and exterminate such affronts to Him on Earth with great prejudice, wherever they attempt to hide from His light.

And yet… exceptions not only exist within the teeming ranks of House Cawdor, but could even be called common. Many denizens of Cawdor are lame of body or weak of wit. Many are abnormally large or strangely proportioned and peculiar to behold. How it is that such variation from the accepted baseline norm of humanity can be tolerated within a House that claims to despise such variations is something of a mystery, but to the Cawdor themselves the answer is simply one of faith. If their leaders choose to allow these souls to live, then live they will, just like any other Cawdor, dedicating their lives to the holy cause. A common sight amongst the peoples of House Cawdor is that of the physically frail and the weak of mind coexisting, working together to do for one another that which they cannot do alone. Sometimes regarded as bearers of stigma, sometimes called 'stigs' amongst the gangs of House Cawdor, but never 'mutants', lest the speaker wish to provoke a violent reaction, these combinations of shambling, slack-jawed behemoth and shrewd-yet-wizened rider can be a great asset to any Cawdor gang seeking to establish dominance in the underhive.

Truly, House Cawdor is home to some strange sights indeed!

M	WS	BS	S	T	W	I	A	Ld	Cl	Wil	Int
4"	4+	4+	5	4	4	4+	2	9+	8+	9+	8+

Weapons	Rng S	Rng L	Acc S	Acc L	S	AP	D	Am	Traits
Heavy club	-	E	-	-	S	-	2	-	Melee
Polearm	E	2"	-	-	S+1	-	1	-	Melee, Unwieldy, Versatile
Heavy stubber	20"	40"	-	-1	4	-1	1	4+	Rapid Fire (2), Unwieldy
Twin-linked heavy stubber	20"	40"	-	-1	4	-1	2	4+	Rapid Fire (3), Unwieldy
Heavy flamer	-	T	-	-	5	-2	1	5+	Blaze, Template, Unwieldy

WEAPONS

A Cawdor Stig-shambler is armed with a heavy club and a heavy stubber.

OPTIONS

- A Cawdor Stig-shambler may upgrade its heavy club with a polearm..Free
- A Cawdor Stig-shambler may upgrade its heavy stubber to
  a twin-linked heavy stubber..+40 credits
- A Cawdor Stig-shambler may upgrade its heavy stubber to
  a heavy flamer...+70 credits
- A Cawdor Stig-shambler may take flak armour ....+10 credits

SPECIAL RULES

Intelligent Control: This fighter may immediately re-roll any failed Leadership, Cool, Willpower or Intelligence check.

Move and Shoot: This fighter may fire an Unwieldy weapon as a Basic action rather than a Double action. However, doing so confers an additional -1 to hit modifier.

Twin-linked Heavy Stubber: When this fighter makes a ranged attack, they may re-roll any number of the Ammo dice rolled. However, they must accept the result of the re-roll, even if it is worse.

GRUNT AND SNIVELS
THE CANDLEKIN
HOUSE CAWDOR

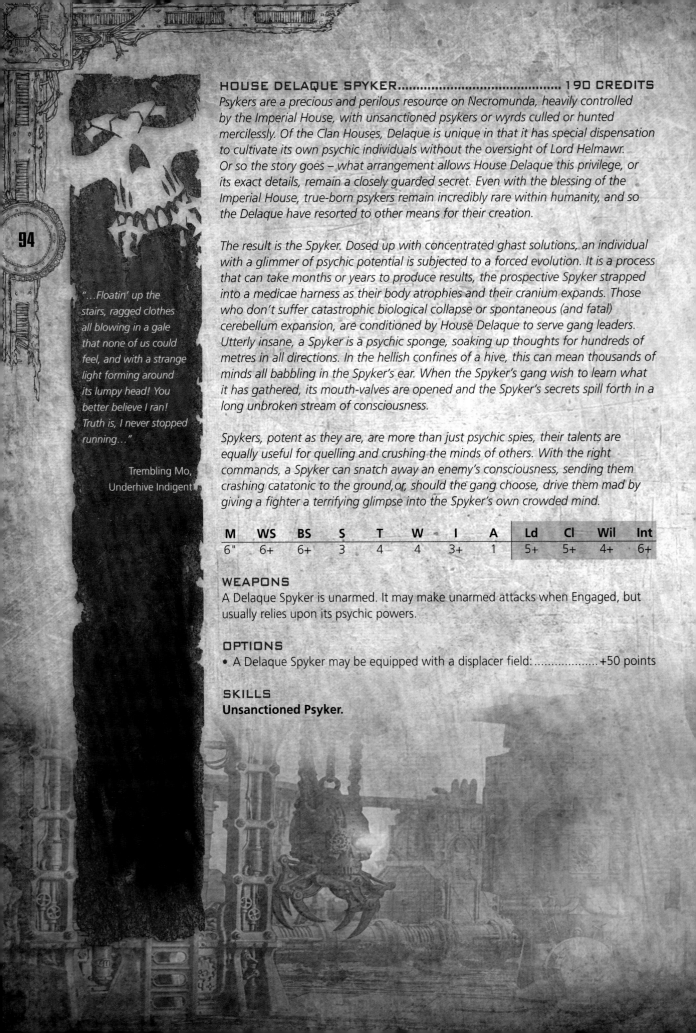

HOUSE DELAQUE SPYKER.. 190 CREDITS

Psykers are a precious and perilous resource on Necromunda, heavily controlled by the Imperial House, with unsanctioned psykers or wyrds culled or hunted mercilessly. Of the Clan Houses, Delaque is unique in that it has special dispensation to cultivate its own psychic individuals without the oversight of Lord Helmawr. Or so the story goes – what arrangement allows House Delaque this privilege, or its exact details, remain a closely guarded secret. Even with the blessing of the Imperial House, true-born psykers remain incredibly rare within humanity, and so the Delaque have resorted to other means for their creation.

The result is the Spyker. Dosed up with concentrated ghast solutions, an individual with a glimmer of psychic potential is subjected to a forced evolution. It is a process that can take months or years to produce results, the prospective Spyker strapped into a medicae harness as their body atrophies and their cranium expands. Those who don't suffer catastrophic biological collapse or spontaneous (and fatal) cerebellum expansion, are conditioned by House Delaque to serve gang leaders. Utterly insane, a Spyker is a psychic sponge, soaking up thoughts for hundreds of metres in all directions. In the hellish confines of a hive, this can mean thousands of minds all babbling in the Spyker's ear. When the Spyker's gang wish to learn what it has gathered, its mouth-valves are opened and the Spyker's secrets spill forth in a long unbroken stream of consciousness.

Spykers, potent as they are, are more than just psychic spies, their talents are equally useful for quelling and crushing the minds of others. With the right commands, a Spyker can snatch away an enemy's consciousness, sending them crashing catatonic to the ground, or, should the gang choose, drive them mad by giving a fighter a terrifying glimpse into the Spyker's own crowded mind.

"...Floatin' up the stairs, ragged clothes all blowing in a gale that none of us could feel, and with a strange light forming around its lumpy head! You better believe I ran! Truth is, I never stopped running..."

Trembling Mo,
Underhive Indigent

M	WS	BS	S	T	W	I	A	Ld	Cl	Wil	Int
6"	6+	6+	3	4	4	3+	1	5+	5+	4+	6+

WEAPONS

A Delaque Spyker is unarmed. It may make unarmed attacks when Engaged, but usually relies upon its psychic powers.

OPTIONS

• A Delaque Spyker may be equipped with a displacer field:...................+50 points

SKILLS

Unsanctioned Psyker.

SPECIAL RULES

Flight: A Spyker ignores all terrain, may move freely between levels without restriction, and can never fall. It may not, however, ignore impassable terrain and may not end its movement with its base overlapping an obstacle or another fighter's base.

WYRD POWERS

TELEPATHY

Psychic Scream (Basic): Any enemy fighters within 3" of this Psyker must immediately pass a Nerve test, subtracting 1 from the result. Any enemy fighter that fails this test is immediately Broken and runs for cover.

Psychic Assault (Basic): Nominate an enemy fighter anywhere within 18" of this Psyker. The nominated fighter must immediately take a Willpower check. If the check is passed, the fighter is Pinned. If the test is failed, the fighter loses 1 Wound and is Pinned. If this reduces the fighter to 0 Wounds, roll one Injury dice and apply the result.

TELEKINESIS

Force Blast (Basic): Any enemy fighters within 3" of this Psyker are immediately pushed D3+1" directly away. If this movement would push a fighter from a platform or into a pitfall, stop at the edge and take an Initiative test for them. If the test is passed, they are placed prone at the edge. If the test is failed, they will fall. If this movement is interrupted by a wall, or other impassable terrain, the fighter is immediately Pinned and takes a hit with a Strength equal to the number of inches rolled for the push distance.

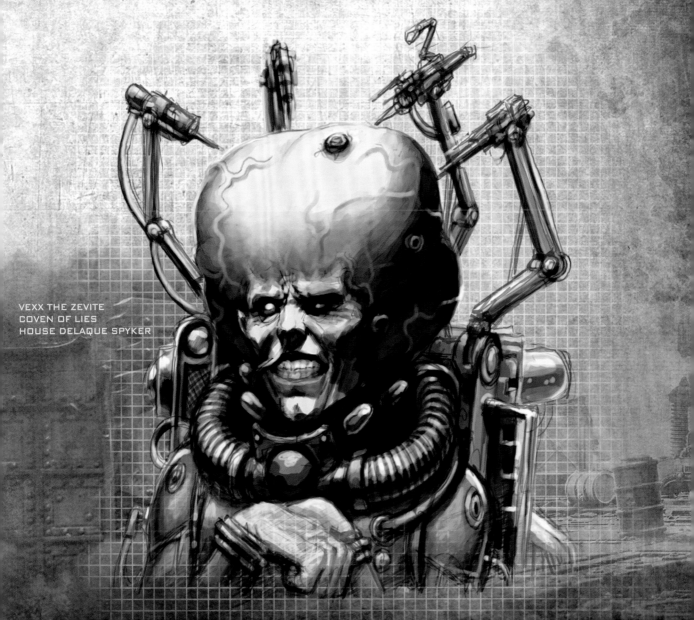

VEXX THE ZEVITE
COVEN OF LIES
HOUSE DELAQUE SPYKER

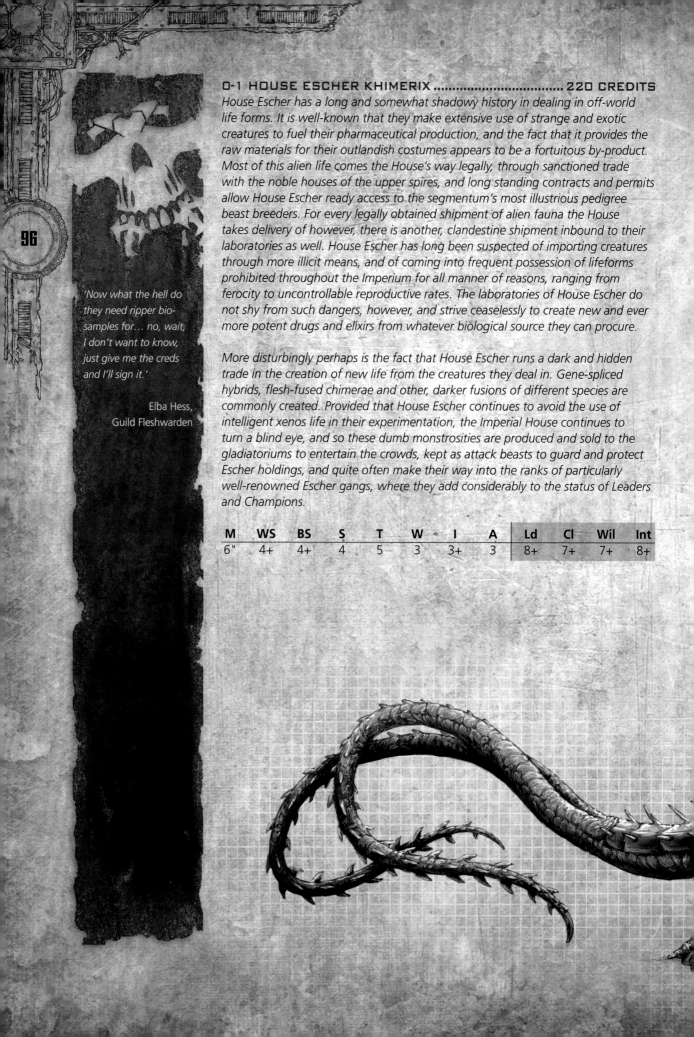

0-1 HOUSE ESCHER KHIMERIX .... 220 CREDITS

*House Escher has a long and somewhat shadowy history in dealing in off-world
life forms. It is well-known that they make extensive use of strange and exotic
creatures to fuel their pharmaceutical production, and the fact that it provides the
raw materials for their outlandish costumes appears to be a fortuitous by-product.
Most of this alien life comes the House's way legally, through sanctioned trade
with the noble houses of the upper spires, and long standing contracts and permits
allow House Escher ready access to the segmentum's most illustrious pedigree
beast breeders. For every legally obtained shipment of alien fauna the House
takes delivery of however, there is another, clandestine shipment inbound to their
laboratories as well. House Escher has long been suspected of importing creatures
through more illicit means, and of coming into frequent possession of lifeforms
prohibited throughout the Imperium for all manner of reasons, ranging from
ferocity to uncontrollable reproductive rates. The laboratories of House Escher do
not shy from such dangers, however, and strive ceaselessly to create new and ever
more potent drugs and elixirs from whatever biological source they can procure.*

*More disturbingly perhaps is the fact that House Escher runs a dark and hidden
trade in the creation of new life from the creatures they deal in. Gene-spliced
hybrids, flesh-fused chimerae and other, darker fusions of different species are
commonly created. Provided that House Escher continues to avoid the use of
intelligent xenos life in their experimentation, the Imperial House continues to
turn a blind eye, and so these dumb monstrosities are produced and sold to the
gladiatoriums to entertain the crowds, kept as attack beasts to guard and protect
Escher holdings, and quite often make their way into the ranks of particularly
well-renowned Escher gangs, where they add considerably to the status of Leaders
and Champions.*

M	WS	BS	S	T	W	I	A	Ld	Cl	Wil	Int
6"	4+	4+	4	5	3	3+	3	8+	7+	7+	8+

Weapon	Rng S	Rng L	Acc S	Acc L	S	AP	D	Am	Traits
Chemical cloud breath weapon	6"	12"	+1	-	3	-1	1	-	Blast (3")
Gaseous eruption breath weapon	-	T	-	-	-	-	-	-	Gas, Template
Talons	-	E	-	-	S	-1	2	-	Melee, Pulverise
Razor-sharp talons	-	E	-	-	S+1	-2	3	-	Melee, Rending

WEAPONS

An Escher Khimerix is armed with a chemical cloud breath weapon and talons.

OPTIONS

- An Escher Khimerix may replace its chemical cloud breath weapon with a gaseous eruption breath weapon .... +80 credits
- An Escher Khimerix may upgrade its talons to razor-sharp talons .... +30 credits
- An Escher Khimerix may have a toughened or scaly hide which counts as flak armour .... +10 credits

SPECIAL RULES

Regeneration: Unless this fighter has a Blaze marker on it, an Escher Khimerix may perform the following action:

Regeneration (Simple) – Roll a D6. On a 4+, this fighter immediately heals one lost wound.

Crushing Blow: Before rolling to hit for this fighter's close combat attacks, the controlling player can nominate one dice to make a Crushing Blow. If that dice hits, the attack's Strength and Damage are each increased by one.

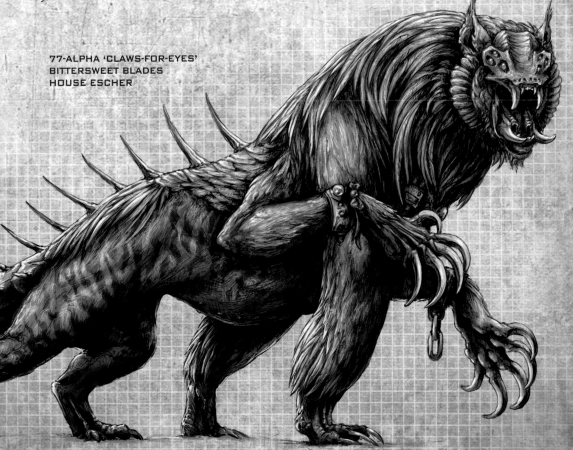

77-ALPHA 'CLAWS-FOR-EYES'
BITTERSWEET BLADES
HOUSE ESCHER

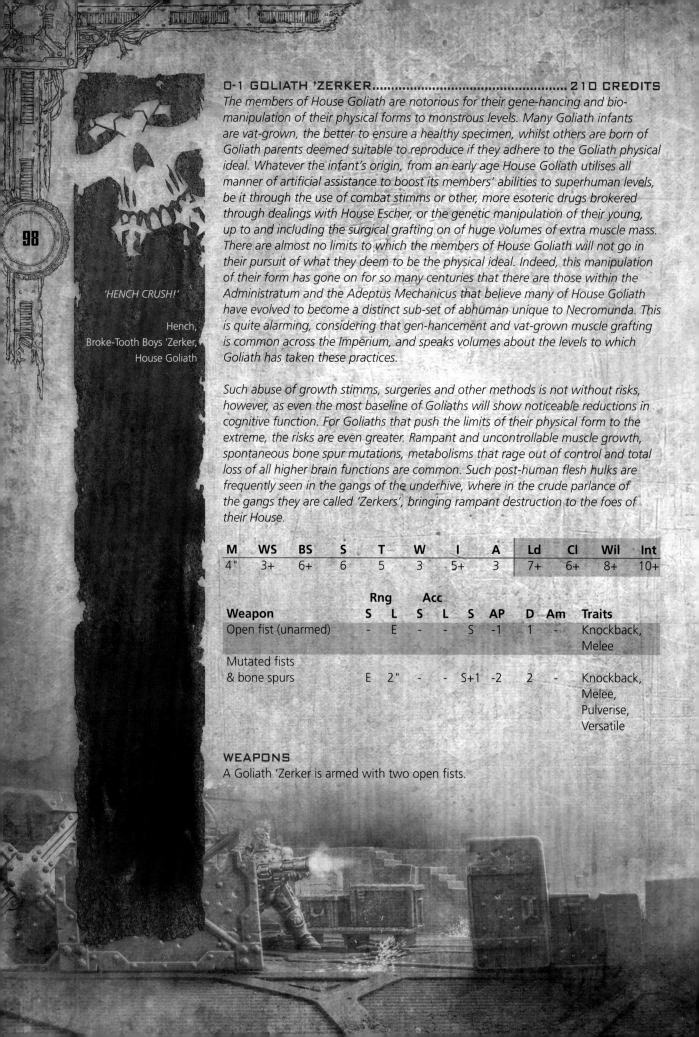

'HENCH CRUSH!'

Hench,
Broke-Tooth Boys 'Zerker,
House Goliath

0-1 GOLIATH 'ZERKER.. 210 CREDITS

The members of House Goliath are notorious for their gene-hancing and bio-manipulation of their physical forms to monstrous levels. Many Goliath infants are vat-grown, the better to ensure a healthy specimen, whilst others are born of Goliath parents deemed suitable to reproduce if they adhere to the Goliath physical ideal. Whatever the infant's origin, from an early age House Goliath utilises all manner of artificial assistance to boost its members' abilities to superhuman levels, be it through the use of combat stimms or other, more esoteric drugs brokered through dealings with House Escher, or the genetic manipulation of their young, up to and including the surgical grafting on of huge volumes of extra muscle mass. There are almost no limits to which the members of House Goliath will not go in their pursuit of what they deem to be the physical ideal. Indeed, this manipulation of their form has gone on for so many centuries that there are those within the Administratum and the Adeptus Mechanicus that believe many of House Goliath have evolved to become a distinct sub-set of abhuman unique to Necromunda. This is quite alarming, considering that gen-hancement and vat-grown muscle grafting is common across the Imperium, and speaks volumes about the levels to which Goliath has taken these practices.

Such abuse of growth stimms, surgeries and other methods is not without risks, however, as even the most baseline of Goliaths will show noticeable reductions in cognitive function. For Goliaths that push the limits of their physical form to the extreme, the risks are even greater. Rampant and uncontrollable muscle growth, spontaneous bone spur mutations, metabolisms that rage out of control and total loss of all higher brain functions are common. Such post-human flesh hulks are frequently seen in the gangs of the underhive, where in the crude parlance of the gangs they are called 'Zerkers', bringing rampant destruction to the foes of their House.

M	WS	BS	S	T	W	I	A	Ld	Cl	Wil	Int
4"	3+	6+	6	5	3	5+	3	7+	6+	8+	10+

	Rng		Acc						
Weapon	**S**	**L**	**S**	**L**	**S**	**AP**	**D**	**Am**	**Traits**
Open fist (unarmed)	-	E	-	-	S	-1	1	-	Knockback, Melee
Mutated fists & bone spurs	E	2"	-	-	S+1	-2	2	-	Knockback, Melee, Pulverise, Versatile

WEAPONS
A Goliath 'Zerker is armed with two open fists.

OPTIONS
- A Goliath 'Zerker may take mutated fists & bone spurs.. +70 credits
- A Goliath 'Zerker may take furnace plate armour... +10 credits
- A Goliath 'Zerker may take a stimm slug stash... +20 credits

SPECIAL RULES
Combat Drug Stash: Whenever this fighter is chosen to make an action, it may choose to use Combat Drugs. Until the end of the turn, this fighter gains an additional +D3 Attacks. However, if the dice roll is a natural 1, the fighter instead suffers a bad reaction and its Attacks characteristic is reduced to 1 until the End phase of this round.

Impetuous: When this fighter Consolidates at the end of a close combat, they can move up to 4" instead of up to 2".

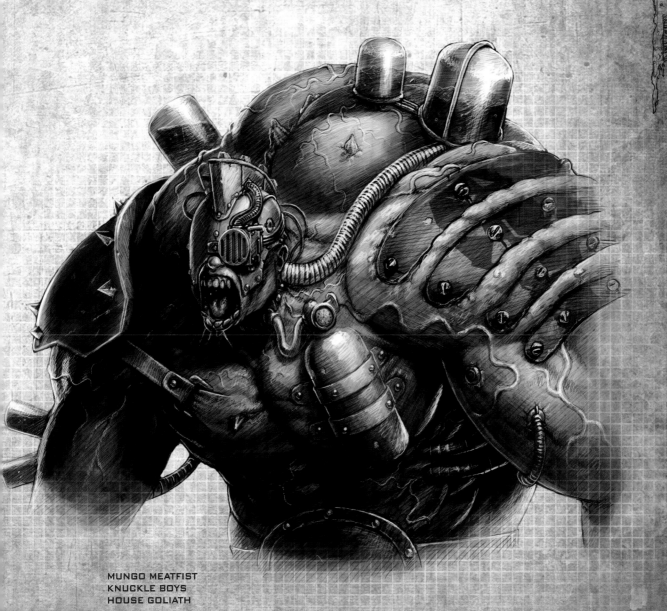

MUNGO MEATFIST
KNUCKLE BOYS
HOUSE GOLIATH

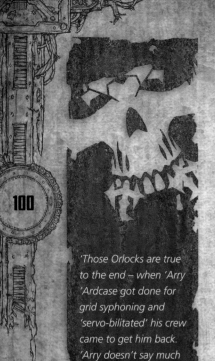

O-1 ORLOCK 'LUGGER' CARGO SERVITOR.............. 230 CREDITS

Common across all of the worlds of the Imperium, servitors are melds of flesh and machine, most often human flesh, but sometimes, as in the case of the Ambot, alien life forms slaved to a servitor engine. Most often, the human component of a servitor is harvested from a convicted criminal, one whose crimes are deemed too great to allow them to carry on as a part of Imperial society but who may continue to serve in another form rather than be wasted in incarceration or execution. Servitors possess the most rudimentary of human intelligence, their minds scrubbed of past memories and all but the most essential knowledge, artificial memory engrams grafted in their place so that they will know their designated role and function and little else. Servitors are put to work in all manner of industry and for any menial task with which an unmodified human cannot be trusted. They work in hostile environments, their living flesh variously blasted by extremes of heat and cold, eroded by extreme elements, or withered and wasted by toxic surroundings, performing their tasks until they fail, at which point their mechanics are reclaimed and a new human donor grafted into place.

House Orlock has ready access to mining and heavy industry servitors of all makes and manner, but those repurposed for gang warfare often take the form referred to by the gangers as 'Luggers' – heavy tracked units able to lift, move and carry bulky cargos. Be they liberated from mine workings or cargo depots, such constructs are well-suited to a combat role with minimal reprogramming.

M	WS	BS	S	T	W	I	A	Ld	Cl	Wil	Int
4"	5+	4+	5	5	3	5+	2	7+	5+	9+	8+

Weapon	Rng S	Rng L	Acc S	Acc L	S	AP	D	Am	Traits
Harpoon launcher	6"	18"	+2	-	5	-3	1	5+	Drag, Impale, Scarce
Heavy bolter	18"	36"	+1	-	5	-2	2	6+	Rapid Fire (2), Unwieldy
Heavy flamer	-	T	-	-	5	-2	1	5+	Blaze, Template, Unwieldy
Heavy stubber	20"	40"	-	-1	4	-1	1	4+	Rapid Fire (2), Unwieldy
Servitor combat weapon	-	E	-	-	S	-1	1	-	Knockback, Melee

WEAPONS

A Lugger is armed with a harpoon launcher.

OPTIONS

- A Lugger may replace its harpoon launcher with a:
  - Heavy bolter..+50 credits
  - Heavy flamer...+85 credits
  - Heavy stubber...+20 credits
- A Lugger may upgrade its light carapace armour to heavy carapace armour ....+20 credits
- A Lugger may take a mono-sight[†]...+25 credits

SPECIAL RULES

Mechanical Construction: A Lugger is equipped with light carapace armour.

Weapons Platform: An unwieldy ranged weapon mounted on a servitor is far more manoeuvrable. When a Lugger fires an Unwieldy ranged weapon, it becomes a Basic action rather than a Double action.

Ammo Hoppers: A Lugger can re-roll any failed Ammo checks that roll a natural 1.

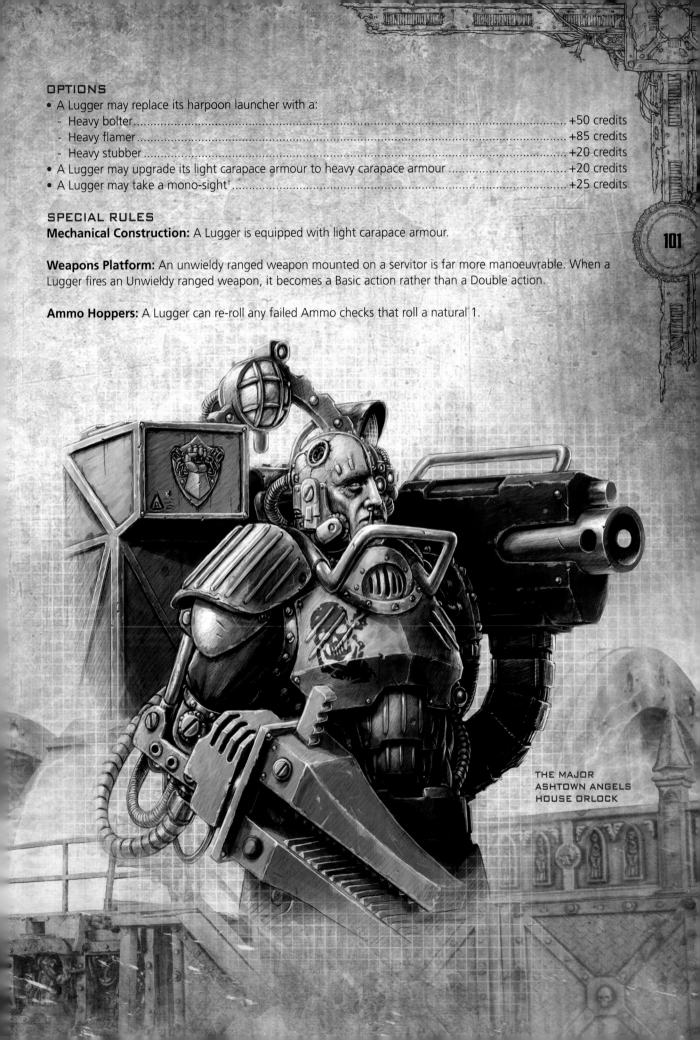

THE MAJOR
ASHTOWN ANGELS
HOUSE ORLOCK

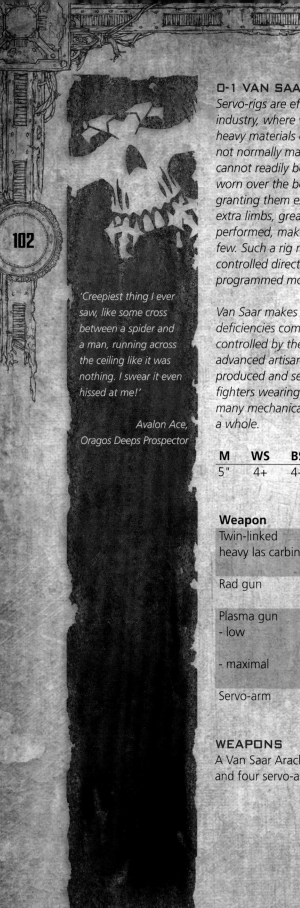

'Creepiest thing I ever saw, like some cross between a spider and a man, running across the ceiling like it was nothing. I swear it even hissed at me!'

Avalon Ace,
Oragos Deeps Prospector

O-1 VAN SAAR 'ARACHNI-RIG' SERVO-SUIT............... 240 CREDITS

Servo-rigs are effectively a mechanical exoskeleton, most commonly seen in heavy industry, where workers may be equipped with them to aid with lifting and moving heavy materials or operating large tools or machinery – anywhere where weights not normally manageable by baseline humans must be handled, but where duties cannot readily be entrusted to abhumans or servitors. Where most servo-rigs are worn over the body and limbs, controlled by the wearer's physical movements and granting them extra strength, servo-rigs are often also utilised to give a worker extra limbs, greatly increasing their dexterity and the range of tasks that can be performed, making what may otherwise be the work of many, the work of a few. Such a rig may be plugged directly into the wearer's nervous system and controlled directly, or may be automated, forcing a worker to keep up with the pre-programmed movements of the rig into which they are strapped.

Van Saar makes particular use of such things, in no small part due to the physical deficiencies common within their House. Very advanced forms of servo harness, controlled by the wearer's nervous system or via a direct MIU are common, advanced artisan pieces that put to shame the simple utilitarian forms mass produced and seen in wide use. In battle, it is not uncommon to see Van Saar fighters wearing massive rigs that grant them a huge, spider-like appearance, with many mechanical limbs that greatly increase the combat efficiency of the gang as a whole.

M	WS	BS	S	T	W	I	A	Ld	Cl	Wil	Int
5"	4+	4+	5	4	3	4+	4	5+	5+	8+	6+

	Rng		Acc						
Weapon	**S**	**L**	**S**	**L**	**S**	**AP**	**D**	**Am**	**Traits**
Twin-linked heavy las carbine	15"	30"	+1	-	4	-	1	4+	Plentiful, Rapid Fire (3)
Rad gun	-	T	-	-	2	-2	1	4+	Rad-phage, Template
Plasma gun - low	12"	24"	+2	-	5	-1	2	5+	Rapid Fire (1), Scarce
- maximal	12"	24"	+1	-	7	-2	3	5+	Scarce, Unstable
Servo-arm	E	3	-	+1	S	-	1	-	Melee, Versatile

WEAPONS

A Van Saar Arachni-rig Servo-suit is armed with a twin-linked heavy las carbine and four servo-arms.

OPTIONS

- A Van Saar Arachni-rig Servo-suit may replace one servo-arm with a rad gun. Doing so will reduce its Attacks characteristic by 1 .... +60 credits
- A Van Saar Arachni-rig Servo-suit may replace one servo-arm with a plasma gun. Doing so will reduce its Attacks characteristic by 1 .... +60 credits
- A Van Saar Arachni-rig Servo-suit may upgrade its light carapace armour to heavy carapace armour .... +20 credits

SPECIAL RULES

Twin-linked Las Carbines: When this fighter makes a ranged attack, they may re-roll any number of the Ammo dice rolled. However, they must accept the result of the re-roll, even if it is worse.

Mechanical Construction: A Van Saar Arachni-rig Servo-suit is equipped with light carapace armour.

Van Saar Protective Gear: Van Saar fighters are somewhat protected from the effects of their own rad weapons by their armour and are therefore immune to the effects of the Rad-phage Weapon Trait (i.e., they will not suffer the additional Flesh Wound).

Superior Weapons Array: Rather than making a single Shoot (Basic) action each turn, this fighter may make two Shoot (Simple) actions per turn. Each action may be made with a different weapon, and each action may target a different enemy fighter, provided that all of the normal rules for Target Priority are followed.

HEISEN 'OCTAVIUM'
THE NEXUS NINES
HOUSE VAN SAAR

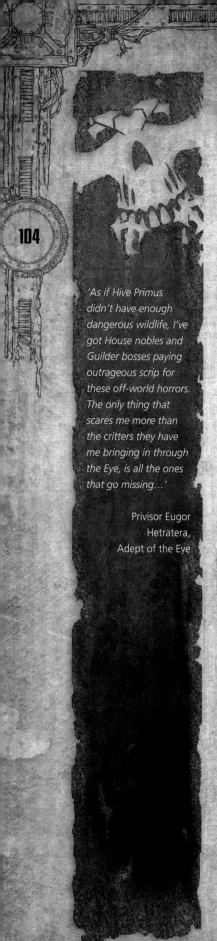

EXOTIC BEASTS

The worlds of the Imperium are host to many strange and wonderful creatures, and Necromunda is no exception. It is well documented throughout the ages that humans have a strange propensity for keeping all manner of creatures as pets, fascinated by their behaviour and comforted by their loyalty, and in this the denizens of the underhive are no different to humans anywhere else in the galaxy. What is unique to Necromunda, though, is the type and variety of pets that people choose to keep…

Exotic Beasts are only available to gang Leaders and Champions. They are purchased as Wargear and should be recorded on their owner's Fighter card accordingly. However, where Exotic Beasts differ to normal Wargear is that they will have their own Fighter card, which details their unique stats, skills, and weaponry. They follow all of the normal rules for a fighter, with the following exceptions:

- Whenever the fighter that owns the Exotic Beast is selected for a scenario, the Exotic Beast may also be deployed. This may take the number of fighters in a starting crew above the number specified by the scenario.
- Whenever the owner of an Exotic Beast activates, the Exotic Beast will activate at the same time if it has been taken.
- Exotic Beasts must always end their activation within 3" of their owner. If the Exotic Beast is more than 3" away at the end of its activation, it must pass a Nerve test or become Broken.
- Should an Exotic Beast become Broken, it will run towards its owner when activated rather than for cover. When an Exotic Beast makes a Running for Cover (Double) action, it runs towards its owner. It is only concerned with getting back within 3" of its owner.
- An Exotic Beast that has become Broken automatically rallies if it ends an activation within 3" of its owner.
- If the owner is removed from the battlefield for any reason, the Exotic Beast is also removed from play.
- If an Exotic Beast is removed from the battlefield for any reason, it is not counted for the purposes of Bottle tests.
- Exotic Beasts gain Experience and suffer Lasting Injuries as a normal Ganger and may become a Specialist. However, due to their nature, the variety of skills available to them as a Specialist is much reduced compared to any other gang fighter. Therefore, Exotic Beasts have their own Skill table on the page opposite.
- Exotic Beasts may not take any additional equipment. They may not use weapons other than those detailed on their profile. They may never use Wargear.
- Exotic Beasts can be taken Captive, in which case the owning fighter's gang can attempt to rescue them and the capturing gang may sell them as if they were a normal fighter. Exotic Beasts taken Captive cannot be put to work in any Territories.

EXOTIC BEAST SKILLS

By their very nature, Exotic Beasts are unable to utilise many of the skills detailed in the complete skill lists. Therefore, when an Exotic Beast gains a new skill, roll a D3 and consult the table below:

D3	Agility	Brawn	Combat	Cunning	Ferocity
1	Catfall	Bull Charge	Counter-attack	Backstab	Berserker
2	Dodge	Crushing Blow	Disarm	Evade	Fearsome
3	Sprint	Iron Jaw	Step Aside	Lie Low	Nerves of Steel

SKILL ACCESS

Exotic Beasts have access to the following skills sets:

	Agility	Brawn	Combat	Cunning	Ferocity
Sheen bird	Secondary	-	-	-	Primary
Cephalopod Spekter	Secondary	-	-	Primary	-
Phyrr Cat	Primary	-	-	Secondary	-
Sumpkroc	-	Primary	-	-	Secondary
Cyber-mastiff	-	-	Primary	-	Secondary
Cyberachnid	Secondary	-	-	Primary	-
Caryatid	Primary	-	-	Secondary	-

OLD SCARTOOTH
CYBER-MASTIFF
HOUSE ORLOCK

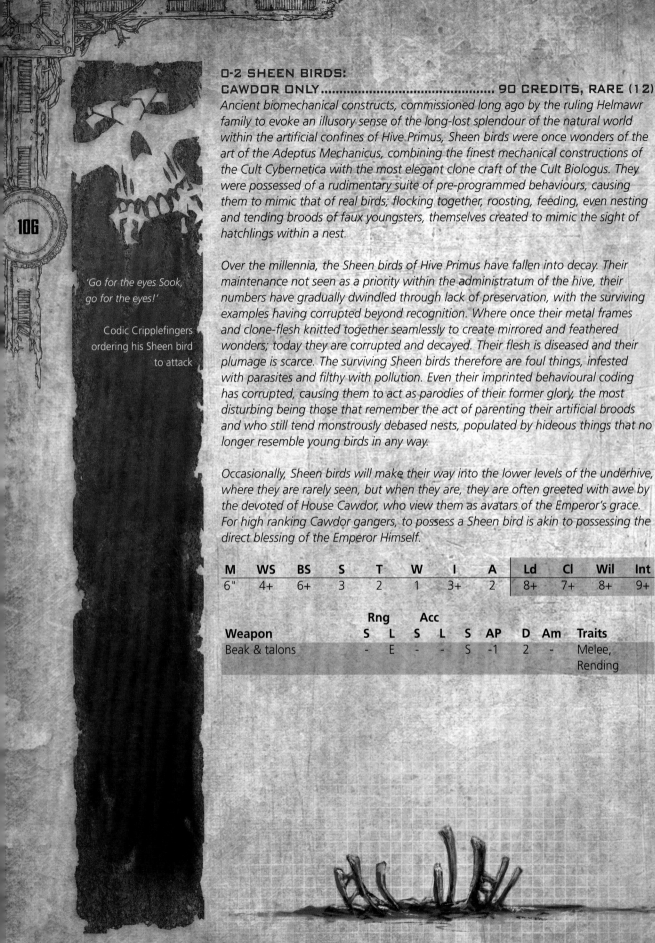

'Go for the eyes Sook, go for the eyes!'

Codic Cripplefingers ordering his Sheen bird to attack

0-2 SHEEN BIRDS:
CAWDOR ONLY .... 90 CREDITS, RARE (12)

Ancient biomechanical constructs, commissioned long ago by the ruling Helmawr family to evoke an illusory sense of the long-lost splendour of the natural world within the artificial confines of Hive Primus, Sheen birds were once wonders of the art of the Adeptus Mechanicus, combining the finest mechanical constructions of the Cult Cybernetica with the most elegant clone craft of the Cult Biologus. They were possessed of a rudimentary suite of pre-programmed behaviours, causing them to mimic that of real birds; flocking together, roosting, feeding, even nesting and tending broods of faux youngsters, themselves created to mimic the sight of hatchlings within a nest.

Over the millennia, the Sheen birds of Hive Primus have fallen into decay. Their maintenance not seen as a priority within the administratum of the hive, their numbers have gradually dwindled through lack of preservation, with the surviving examples having corrupted beyond recognition. Where once their metal frames and clone-flesh knitted together seamlessly to create mirrored and feathered wonders; today they are corrupted and decayed. Their flesh is diseased and their plumage is scarce. The surviving Sheen birds therefore are foul things, infested with parasites and filthy with pollution. Even their imprinted behavioural coding has corrupted, causing them to act as parodies of their former glory, the most disturbing being those that remember the act of parenting their artificial broods and who still tend monstrously debased nests, populated by hideous things that no longer resemble young birds in any way.

Occasionally, Sheen birds will make their way into the lower levels of the underhive, where they are rarely seen, but when they are, they are often greeted with awe by the devoted of House Cawdor, who view them as avatars of the Emperor's grace. For high ranking Cawdor gangers, to possess a Sheen bird is akin to possessing the direct blessing of the Emperor Himself.

M	WS	BS	S	T	W	I	A	Ld	Cl	Wil	Int
6"	4+	6+	3	2	1	3+	2	8+	7+	8+	9+

Weapon	Rng S	Rng L	Acc S	Acc L	S	AP	D	Am	Traits
Beak & talons	-	E	-	-	S	-1	2	-	Melee, Rending

SPECIAL RULES

Flight: A Sheen bird ignores all terrain, may move freely between levels without restriction, and can never fall. It may not, however, ignore impassable terrain and may not end its movement with its base overlapping an obstacle or another fighter's base.

Bate: When the owning fighter activates, the Sheen bird will attempt to charge an enemy fighter even if the owning fighter does not wish it to. Make a Willpower check for the owning fighter, if this test is failed, the Sheen bird must attempt to charge the closest enemy fighter. If the check is passed, the Sheen bird activates as normal.

Rake Away: At the end of the Sheen bird's activation, if the owner is Standing and Active or Prone and Pinned, they may choose to make a Willpower check. If this check is passed, the Sheen bird will immediately make a free Move (Simple) action, or Retreat (Basic) action if Engaged, directly towards the owner. If the check is failed, the Sheen bird does not make this free action and stays where it is.

MARROWPICKER
HOUSE CAWDOR SHEEN BIRD

'Is there anything as dismal in all of Hive Primus as the Sheen birds? Another failed experiment by our much lauded ancestors that we are forced to live with. Of all of the hive's populace it seems only the unfortunates of House Cawdor take any real notice of them – perhaps because all that faded finery and failed promise reminds them of their own warped belief system.'

Vivver Ran Lo,
Lord of the Menageries,
Hive Primus

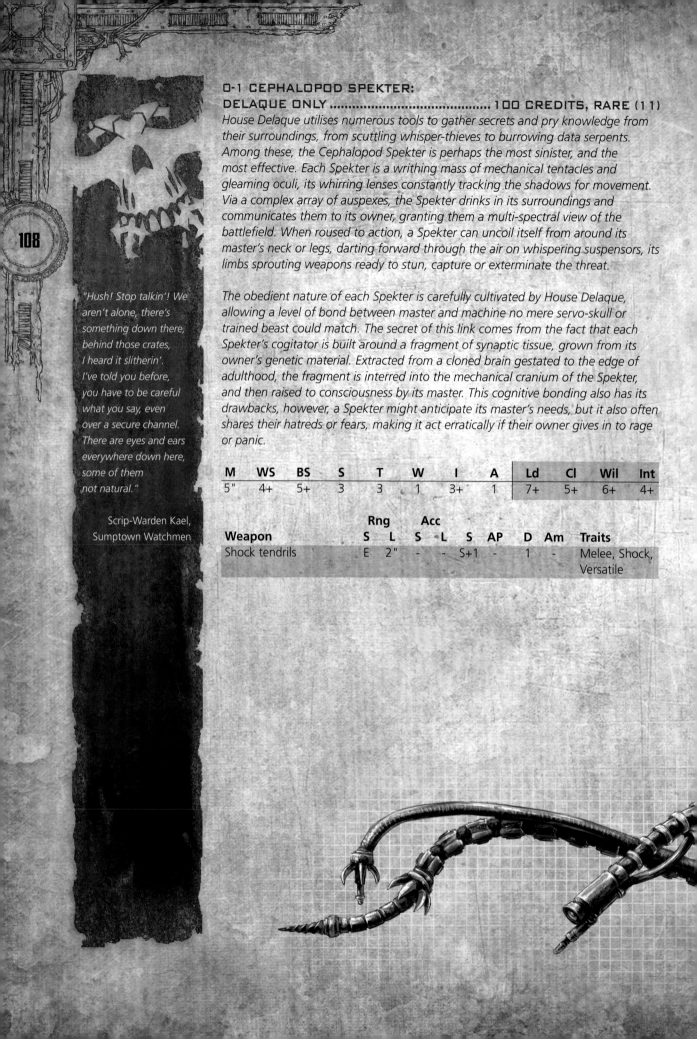

0-1 CEPHALOPOD SPEKTER:
DELAQUE ONLY .... 100 CREDITS, RARE (11)

House Delaque utilises numerous tools to gather secrets and pry knowledge from their surroundings, from scuttling whisper-thieves to burrowing data serpents. Among these, the Cephalopod Spekter is perhaps the most sinister, and the most effective. Each Spekter is a writhing mass of mechanical tentacles and gleaming oculi, its whirring lenses constantly tracking the shadows for movement. Via a complex array of auspexes, the Spekter drinks in its surroundings and communicates them to its owner, granting them a multi-spectral view of the battlefield. When roused to action, a Spekter can uncoil itself from around its master's neck or legs, darting forward through the air on whispering suspensors, its limbs sprouting weapons ready to stun, capture or exterminate the threat.

The obedient nature of each Spekter is carefully cultivated by House Delaque, allowing a level of bond between master and machine no mere servo-skull or trained beast could match. The secret of this link comes from the fact that each Spekter's cogitator is built around a fragment of synaptic tissue, grown from its owner's genetic material. Extracted from a cloned brain gestated to the edge of adulthood, the fragment is interred into the mechanical cranium of the Spekter, and then raised to consciousness by its master. This cognitive bonding also has its drawbacks, however, a Spekter might anticipate its master's needs, but it also often shares their hatreds or fears, making it act erratically if their owner gives in to rage or panic.

M	WS	BS	S	T	W	I	A	Ld	Cl	Wil	Int
5"	4+	5+	3	3	1	3+	1	7+	5+	6+	4+

Weapon	Rng S	Rng L	Acc S	Acc L	S	AP	D	Am	Traits
Shock tendrils	E	2"	-	-	S+1	-	1	-	Melee, Shock, Versatile

SPECIAL RULES

Flight: A Cephalopod Spekter ignores all terrain, may move freely between levels without restriction, and can never fall. It may not, however, ignore impassable terrain and may not end its movement with its base overlapping an obstacle or another fighter's base.

Sensor Array: If a Cephalopod Spekter is within 3" of its owner when the owner is required to make an Intelligence check for any reason, roll an extra D6, then pick one of the dice to discard.

Threat Response: If the Cephalopod Spekter's owner is taken Out of Action whilst within 3" of the Cephalopod Spekter, immediately before the Cephalopod Spekter itself is removed from play, all enemy fighters within D6" of the Cephalopod Spekter suffer a Strength 1 automatic hit, as if from a weapon with the Seismic trait.

Watchdog: If the Cephalopod Spekter's owner is a sentry in a scenario that uses the Sentries special rule, they can attempt to spot attackers even if they are not within their vision arc. In addition, the D6 roll to see whether a fighter is spotted has a +1 modifier (a natural 1 still fails).

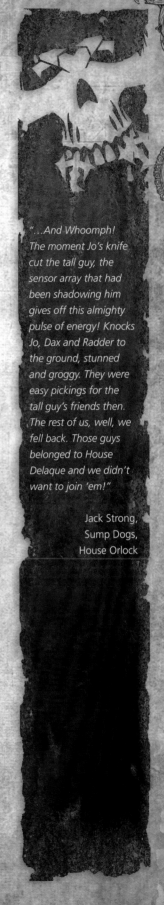

"...And Whoomph! The moment Jo's knife cut the tall guy, the sensor array that had been shadowing him gives off this almighty pulse of energy! Knocks Jo, Dax and Radder to the ground, stunned and groggy. They were easy pickings for the tall guy's friends then. The rest of us, well, we fell back. Those guys belonged to House Delaque and we didn't want to join 'em!"

Jack Strong,
Sump Dogs,
House Orlock

109

SPEKTOR-34 'H4RV3Y'
COVEN OF LIES
HOUSE DELAQUE

O-2 PHYRR CAT:

ESCHER ONLY... 120 CREDITS, RARE (12)

House Escher has a long tradition of dealing in many strange and exotic off-world creatures. At its most basic, this trade in xenos fauna helps to fuel many of their unique elixirs and forms no small part of the basis for their trade and expertise in alchemical technology. A side effect of this prodigious, and often elicit, trade in alien life, is that House Escher has access to the pelts and plumage of many wonderful beasts, and this is clearly evidenced in the Escher style of dress. It is also not uncommon for House Escher to bring onto Necromunda the creatures that feature in the fighting pits and gladiatoriums, a trade which in turn enables the House to set up ever more contacts amongst the many big game hunters and Rogue Traders that specialise in such commodities.

However, not all off-world beasts are destined for the Escher laboratoriums or the fighting pits of Necromunda, some creatures are prized as companions, especially the various felids that originate on many different worlds. Eschers are attracted to the big cats of Phyrr in particular for their exotic looks and killer instincts. Such beasts are rare in the extreme and smuggling them planetside to Hive Primus is no mean feat, so they are an incredibly rare sight as pets even amongst the hierarchy of House Escher. Yet seen they are, and when the opportunity to acquire such a beast, or even better, a mating pair, arises, Esher gang chiefs will go to any lengths to secure them.

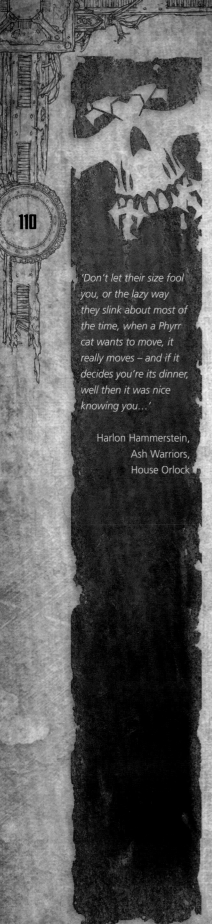

'Don't let their size fool you, or the lazy way they slink about most of the time, when a Phyrr cat wants to move, it really moves – and if it decides you're its dinner, well then it was nice knowing you…'

Harlon Hammerstein,
Ash Warriors,
House Orlock

M	WS	BS	S	T	W	I	A	Ld	Cl	Wil	Int
7"	3+	-	3	3	1	2+	2	7+	8+	7+	8+

Weapon	Range S	Range L	Acc S	Acc L	S	AP	D	Am	Traits
Talons	-	E	-	-	S	-1	2	-	Melee, Pulverise

SPECIAL RULES

Independent: Unlike other Exotic Pets, a Phyrr Cat must always try to remain within 9" of its owner rather than the usual 3".

Lands on her Feet: If a Phyrr Cat falls for any reason, it will always reduce the Strength of the impact by -2.

FLUFFY
PHYRR CAT
HOUSE ESCHER

0-1 SUMPKROC:

GOLIATH ONLY .... **130 CREDITS, RARE (11)**

Hive legend has it that many thousands of years ago, during a different age of Necromunda, a now long-extinct type of reptile became the fashion accessory of choice for uphive nobility. Imported as eggs, once hatched, these snappy little creatures were seen everywhere for a period of several seasons, kept in fine artificial habitats or carried around in specially-made hand luggage. They became almost common, rapidly…

But as they became common, so too did they become big, and with size came increased aggression. Many were culled after accidents led to lost digits, even lost limbs, and in some cases, so the legends go, loss of life. Many more were hurriedly discarded down waste shutes and heat sinks. And so, in the fullness of time, many were found by the denizens of the underhive.

Over time, these strange creatures were captured as a new food source, but that practice ended as they were more likely to make food of their human hunters. And there their story might have ended in extinction, but for the intervention of House Goliath. For some inexplicable reason, the Goliaths were attracted to these creatures as pets, taking pride in their size and strength, and revelling in their ferocity.

Today, the Sumpkrocs that House Goliath keep are somewhat different to the original creature, with centuries of genetic cloning causing a few changes and they no longer wholly resemble the creature first imported…

'A sumpkroc will eat anything if it's starving enough – that's why I like to keep my krocs good and hungry…'

Grinder Jax,
Scrap Lords,
House Goliath

M	WS	BS	S	T	W	I	A	Ld	Cl	Wil	Int
4"	3+	-	4	4	2	6+	2	8+	6+	7+	11+

Weapon	Rng S	Rng L	Acc S	Acc L	S	AP	D	Am	Traits
Ferocious jaws	-	E	-	-	S	-1	1	-	Melee, Rending

SPECIAL RULES

Counter Charge: If the Sumpkroc's owner is Engaged by an enemy fighter as the result of the enemy fighter making a Charge (Double) action, and if the Sumpkroc is Standing and Active, it may immediately activate and make a Charge (Double) action, moving towards the charging enemy fighter. If, at the end of this movement, the Sumpkroc has Engaged the enemy fighter, it may immediately Attack, as normal for a fighter performing a Charge (Double) action. This activation interrupts the enemy fighter's action, being performed after movement but before attacks.

The Sumpkroc may only make one Counter Charge per round.

Scaly Hide: The Sumpkroc has a naturally scaly and resilient hide, granting it a 5+ save roll.

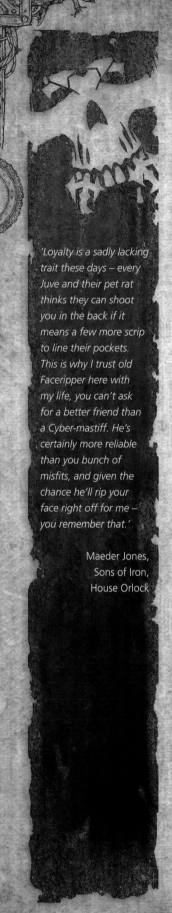

'Loyalty is a sadly lacking trait these days – every Juve and their pet rat thinks they can shoot you in the back if it means a few more scrip to line their pockets. This is why I trust old Faceripper here with my life, you can't ask for a better friend than a Cyber-mastiff. He's certainly more reliable than you bunch of misfits, and given the chance he'll rip your face right off for me – you remember that.'

Maeder Jones,
Sons of Iron,
House Orlock

0-3 CYBER-MASTIFF:

ORLOCK ONLY .... 100 CREDITS, RARE (10)

Mankind has utilised canines for many millennia. From the earliest proto-humans living a primitive existence on Ancient Terra, throughout the great expansion and colonisation of the stars during the Dark Age of Technology and beyond, wherever humanity has gone, it has taken its trusty hound.

Over the millennia, canines have continually evolved. From careful breeding programmes to enhance certain beneficial traits and reduce undesirable qualities, to genhancing and cloning, dogs have in no way been excluded from practices Mankind has proven ready and willing to try upon itself.

On Necromunda, dogs are no less common than anywhere else in the Imperium, though it must be said that they often provide a food source more readily than they provide their traditional roles of companion, guard or hunter. However, they do still have loyal friends amongst the people. Guilders breed and keep large hounds to protect their caravans and holdings, and House Orlock in particular takes great pride in the breeding of dogs as guards and fighters. The dogs of House Orlock show great diversity of type. From the sleek, alert watch dogs they breed to guard their mine workings and store houses, to the stocky, bull-like fighting dogs they breed for sport, Orlock Gangers are frequently accompanied by hounds. What's more, to the outsider there is a strange sentimentality shown by Orlocks towards their dogs, and it is not uncommon to see hounds sporting expensive cybernetics to compensate for past injuries or illness.

M	WS	BS	S	T	W	I	A	Ld	Cl	Wil	Int
5"	3+	-	3	3	1	4+	1	7+	6+	8+	8+

Weapon	Rng S	Rng L	Acc S	Acc L	S	AP	D	Am	Traits
Savage bite	-	E	-	-	S	-2	1	-	Disarm, Melee

SPECIAL RULES

Watchdog: If the Cyber-mastiff's owner is a sentry in a scenario that uses the Sentries special rule, they can attempt to spot attackers even if they are not within their vision arc. In addition, the D6 roll to see whether a fighter is spotted has a +1 modifier (a natural 1 still fails).

Loyal Protector: Whilst the Cyber-mastiff is Standing and either Active or Engaged, and within 3" of its owner, enemy fighters may not make a Coup De Grace action against the owner.

0-3 CYBERACHNID:
VAN SAAR ONLY .... 75 CREDITS, RARE (10)

Spiders are common to every human-colonised world of the galaxy. Perhaps millennia ago, when Mankind set out to populate the stars, those first ships had onboard stowaways in the form of insects and arachnids accidentally introduced to new ecosystems. Perhaps they were deliberately introduced to control dangerous insect life on many worlds. Or perhaps they were always there. No one knows for sure, but that spiders can be found almost everywhere humanity thrives is beyond doubt.

The hives of Necromunda are infamous for their mutant spiders, and many millions of subspecies exist in the dark corners and dusty cracks of the great hives. Some varieties can grow to several feet across, and their presence can make whole domes uninhabitable.

The spiders of Necromunda mean much to the planet, not least featuring heavily in the heraldry of many clans and ruling families. Yet possibly the most readily made association is to the House of Van Saar, whose sigil is the likeness of a spider. Van Saar play on this, capturing and breeding large Necromundan arachnids and modifying them cybernetically for many purposes. Van Saar gangs are often accompanied by several such slaved servitor spiders, and their gruesome appearance is often enough to make the faint-hearted maintain what they feel is a safe distance, but in truth is right in the crosshairs, where the Van Saar want them…

'A Cyberachnid is a finely crafted piece of tech – auspex bafflers and vox casters, venom injectors in pneumatic piston fangs, along with cyclic web throwers and a scuttler rig that can handle dozens of terrain configurations. Also, it looks scary as all hell.'

Elesk Icearch,
Code Wardens,
House Van Saar

M	WS	BS	S	T	W	I	A	Ld	Cl	Wil	Int
6"	4+	5+	2	2	1	2+	1	7+	8+	8+	8+

Weapon	Rng S	Rng L	Acc S	Acc L	S	AP	D	Am	Traits
Venomous bite	-	E	-	-	-	-	-	-	Melee, Toxin
Web projector	-	T	-	-	2	-	-	6+	Scarce, Template, Web

SPECIAL RULES

Clamber: When this fighter climbs, the vertical distance they move is not halved. In other words, they always count as climbing up or down a ladder.

Fear Inducing: Cyberachnids have the Fearsome (Ferocity) skill and may confer this onto their owner. The owner only gains this skill provided they have an Active Cyberachnid within 3", otherwise the skill is lost.

Fearsome (Ferocity) – If an enemy makes a Charge action that targets this fighter, they must make a Willpower check before moving. If the check is failed, they cannot move and their action ends immediately.

Horrific: A Cyberachnid is a horrifying meld of machine and spider that gangers of other Houses would just as soon not have in their hide-out. A Cyberachnid can never be Captured.

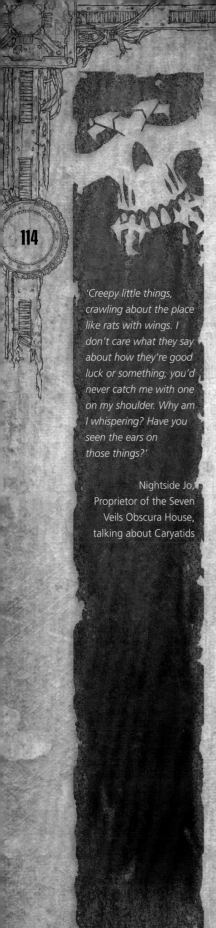

0-1 CARYATID:
AVAILABLE TO ANY GANG LEADER............. 0 CREDITS*, RARE (15)

Caryatids are small, winged, blue humanoid creatures which infest the many air-ducts and vents throughout Necromunda's many hives. They are seen as good luck charms by the majority of hivers for their tendency to attach themselves to charismatic, powerful and successful individuals: for example, very successful and memorable House leaders throughout history have often been attended by Caryatids, and Necromunda's Planetary Governor Lord Helmawr himself is known to have at least one which chooses to keep him constant company.

Mildly psychic, they are particularly attracted to the soon-to-become-powerful and can penetrate human minds, usefully recognising malicious intentions against their companions, further fuelling their reputations as bringers of good luck. However, an individual whose 'pet' Caryatid leaves them is regarded as waiting for death, for as their arrival is considered a good omen, their departure is seen as an omen of doom.

Caryatids' blue skin is generally covered by an intricate, tattoo-like pattern, and some are known to paint their faces, or wear bracelets, bangles, anklets and earrings. It is unknown whether these strange creatures are some manner of mutant, vat-grown organic creatures long ago gone feral, aliens or something altogether more inexplicable, all that is known is that to be selected as the companion of a Caryatid is a great, if fleeting, boon.

M	WS	BS	S	T	W	I	A	Ld	Cl	Wil	Int
6"	5+	-	2	2	1	2+	1	7+	7+	8+	8+

A Caryatid carries no weapons and will always make unarmed attacks.

SPECIAL RULES
Omen of Fortune: A Caryatid is able to sense bad fortune and forewarn its chosen companion, giving them a flash of precognition.

Whilst the Caryatid is within 3" of its owner, that fighter may avoid one successful hit per turn by making a successful Willpower check. Make the check immediately after a successful roll to hit has been made against the fighter. If the check is failed, the attack hits as normal. If the check is passed, the attack counts as having missed and the dice roll is discarded. Templates and Blast markers are placed as normal for the purposes of determining hits against other models, but the Caryatid's owner is assumed to have somehow dodged clear.

Precognition: The gift of foresight possessed by the Caryatid enables it to dodge and evade all but the most unexpected of attacks. This tremendous precognition grants the Caryatid a 3+ save roll, which cannot be modified by Armour Piercing.

Additionally, a Caryatid may avoid being caught by a Blast marker or Flame template. If a Caryatid is caught under a Blast marker or Flame template, the attacker should roll a D6. On a 4-6, the Caryatid is hit by the attack. On a 1-3, the Caryatid is able to fly clear of the area of the attack. Leave the model where it is and assume that it has fluttered around to avoid the attack and returned to where it was.

Symbol of Renown: So long as your gang Leader is accompanied by a Caryatid, the gang's Reputation is increased by +1. However, should the Caryatid ever be killed, or should it ever abandon its companion, the gang's Reputation will be reduced by -2.

Abandonment: Should the gang reduce its Reputation for any reason, roll a D6 and subtract the number of Reputation lost from the result. If the total is 1 or less, the Caryatid will abandon its companion. A natural roll of a 6 is always a success, regardless of modifiers.

Flight: A Caryatid ignores all terrain, may move freely between levels without restriction, and can never fall. It may not, however, ignore impassable terrain and may not end its movement with its base overlapping an obstacle or another fighter's base.

A Caryatid is not purchased like other items of Wargear, instead one may decide of its own volition to make a companion of a gang leader or not.

Should the gang roll 15 or higher after modification when making a Seek Rare Equipment check during the post-battle sequence, there is a chance that a Caryatid will attach itself to the gang Leader. Roll 2D6 and add the gang's current Reputation. If the result is 20 or higher, a Caryatid has decided to form a bond with the gang Leader.

'Caryatids aren't what they seem!'

Popular Hive Primus
Graffiti

115

OMEN OF EYES
CARYATID
ORIGIN UNKNOWN

THE TRADING POST

The Trading Post represents the various markets, traders and caravans where gangs can barter for weapons and equipment. Where the House Equipment Lists provide commonly-used equipment for each House's gangs, the type of arms and armament that gangs will readily be able to lay their hands on, the Trading Post lets them expand their arsenal beyond the norm.

Note that some weapons and Wargear that are found on House Equipment Lists do not appear here; these items are preciously guarded by each House, and are not available on the open market. Furthermore, some items are so intrinsically linked to a certain House that gangers of other Houses would be unwilling or even ashamed to use them even if they could get their hands on them. For example, some of the other Houses view House Van Saar's reliance upon energy-based weapons as a symptom of their inherent weakness, and so they shun las carbines in favour of more robust autoguns.

Also, note that some items are cheaper in the House Equipment Lists, and that some items listed as Rare here are available in the House Equipment Lists; this is intentional, representing the increased availability of those items to specific Houses. Where this is the case, the entry in the House Equipment List takes precedence over the entry shown here for that gang.

Weapons marked with an asterisk (*) take up the space of two weapons. If, for example, a fighter can carry three weapons, any weapon marked with an asterisk counts as two weapons of those three.

Weapon accessories marked with a dagger (†) may not be combined together on the same weapon. If one such accessory is purchased for a weapon, another may not be added.

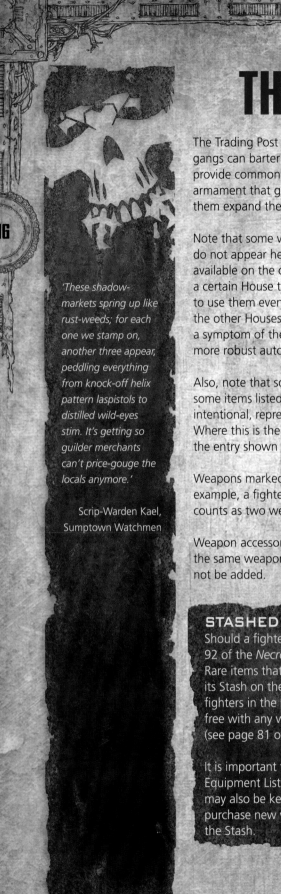

'These shadow-markets spring up like rust-weeds; for each one we stamp on, another three appear, peddling everything from knock-off helix pattern laspistols to distilled wild-eyes stim. It's getting so guilder merchants can't price-gouge the locals anymore.'

Scrip-Warden Kael,
Sumptown Watchmen

STASHED WEAPONS AND WARGEAR

Should a fighter die, their weapons and Wargear might not be lost (see page 92 of the *Necromunda Rulebook*). Such useful equipment and expensive or Rare items that can be looted will be and are kept by the gang and added to its Stash on the gang roster. These items may be redistributed amongst other fighters in the post-battle sequence, or a new fighter may be equipped for free with any weapons or Wargear held in the gang's Stash when recruited (see page 81 of the *Necromunda Rulebook*).

It is important to note that this is not limited to items contained in the House Equipment List, items purchased through the Trading Post as detailed here may also be kept in the Stash and redistributed in this way. Should any fighter purchase new weapons or Wargear, old weapons or Wargear may be added to the Stash.

WEAPONS
BASIC WEAPONS

Item	Price	Rarity
Autogun	15 credits	Common
Reclaimed autogun	10 credits	Common
Boltgun	55 credits	Rare (8)
Combat shotgun		
- salvo & shredder ammo	70 credits	Rare (7)
- firestorm ammo	30 credits	Rare (8)
Lasgun	15 credits	Common
Sawn-off shotgun	15 credits	Common
Shotgun		
- solid & scatter ammo	30 credits	Common
- executioner ammo	20 credits	Rare (9)
- inferno ammo	15 credits	Rare (8)
Throwing knives	10 credits	Common

PISTOLS

Item	Price	Rarity
Autopistol	10 credits	Common
Reclaimed autopistol	5 credits	Common
Bolt pistol	45 credits	Rare (8)
Combi-pistol		
- autopistol/hand flamer	65 credits	Rare (10)
- autopistol/plasma pistol	50 credits	Rare (10)
- bolt pistol/hand flamer	110 credits	Rare (11)
- bolt pistol/plasma pistol	80 credits	Rare (11)
- stub gun/plasma pistol	40 credits	Rare (8)
Hand flamer	75 credits	Rare (8)
Laspistol	10 credits	Common
Needle pistol	30 credits	Rare (9)
Plasma pistol	50 credits	Rare (9)
Stub gun	5 credits	Common
- dumdum rounds	5 credits	Rare (7)
Web pistol	90 credits	Rare (9)

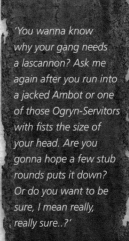

'You wanna know why your gang needs a lascannon? Ask me again after you run into a jacked Ambot or one of those Ogryn-Servitors with fists the size of your head. Are you gonna hope a few stub rounds puts it down? Or do you want to be sure, I mean really, really sure..?'

Honest Cabas,
Cabas' Quality Arms,
Girdercity

'In the Guard there's all these rules and regs about using hardware like this – say your benedictions to the machine, make sure it's secured on the tripod, always stay next to your loader... truth is, if you've got the muscle you don't need any of that. I've seen a ganger hauling about a stripped down heavy bolter, with one hand on the trigger and the other wrapped in ammo belts. And as for prayers to the machine – heck, keep firing until it jams then hit them with the damn thing!'

Kray Vog,
Dust Wall Veteran

SPECIAL WEAPONS

Item	Price	Rarity
Combi-weapon		
- autogun/flamer	110 credits	Rare (10)
- autogun/ grenade launcher (frag)	30 credits	Rare (7)
- bolter/flamer	180 credits	Rare (8)
- bolter/grenade launcher (frag)	60 credits	Rare (8)
- bolter/melta	170 credits	Rare (12)
- bolter/needler	90 credits	Rare (10)
- bolter/plasma	115 credits	Rare (10)
Flamer	140 credits	Rare (7)
Grav-gun	120 credits	Rare (11)
Grenade launcher		
- frag & krak grenades	65 credits	Rare (8)
- choke gas grenades	35 credits	Rare (9)
- photon flash grenades	15 credits	Rare (9)
- scare gas grenades	45 credits	Rare (10)
- smoke gas grenades	15 credits	Common
Long las	20 credits	Common
Long rifle	30 credits	Rare (7)
Meltagun	135 credits	Rare (11)
Needle rifle	40 credits	Rare (9)
Plasma gun	100 credits	Rare (9)
Web gun	125 credits	Rare (9)

HEAVY WEAPONS

Item	Price	Rarity
Harpoon launcher*	110 credits	Rare (9)
Heavy bolter*	160 credits	Rare (10)
Heavy flamer*	195 credits	Rare (10)
Heavy stubber*	130 credits	Rare (7)
Lascannon*	155 credits	Rare (10)
Mining laser*	125 credits	Rare (9)
		Rare (8 Orlock)
Missile launcher (with frag & krak missiles)*	165 credits	Rare (10)
Multi-melta*	180 credits	Rare (11)
Plasma cannon*	130 credits	Rare (11)
Seismic cannon*	140 credits	Rare (10)

CLOSE COMBAT WEAPONS

Item	Price	Rarity
Knives		
Fighting knife	15 credits	Common
Power knife	25 credits	Rare (9)
Stiletto knife	20 credits	Rare (9)
Mundane Combat Weapons		
Axe	10 credits	Common
Chainaxe	30 credits	Rare (9)
Chainsword	25 credits	Rare (8)
Digi laser	25 credits	Rare (10)
Flail	20 credits	Common
Maul (club)	10 credits	Common
Servo claw	35 credits	Rare (10)
Sword	20 credits	Rare (6)
Stiletto sword	35 credits	Rare (9)
Power/Shock Weapons		
Las cutter	85 credits	Rare (10)
Power sword	50 credits	Rare (9)
Power axe	35 credits	Rare (8)
Power hammer	45 credits	Rare (8)
Power pick	40 credits	Rare (8)
Power maul	30 credits	Rare (8)
Shock baton	30 credits	Rare (8)
Shock stave	25 credits	Rare (9)
Thunder hammer	70 credits	Rare (11)
Two-handed Weapons		
Chain glaive*	60 credits	Rare (7)
Heavy rock cutter*	135 credits	Rare (9) Rare (8 Goliath & Orlock)
Heavy rock drill*	90 credits	Rare (9)
Heavy rock saw*	120 credits	Rare (9)
Two-handed axe*	25 credits	Common
Two-handed hammer*	35 credits	Common

'Ain't nothing like the sound of a chainsword starting up – I swear to the Spire when that throaty roar kicks in, every ganger in earshot just soiled themselves.'

Haks 'Blood and Gore' Torlor, Slaughterfists, House Goliath

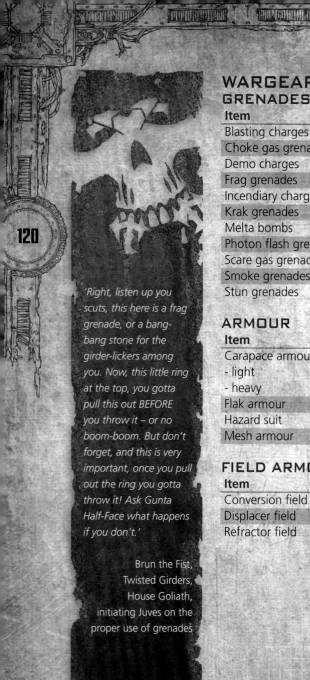

'Right, listen up you scuts, this here is a frag grenade, or a bang-bang stone for the girder-lickers among you. Now, this little ring at the top, you gotta pull this out BEFORE you throw it – or no boom-boom. But don't forget, and this is very important, once you pull out the ring you gotta throw it! Ask Gunta Half-Face what happens if you don't.'

Brun the Fist,
Twisted Girders,
House Goliath,
initiating Juves on the
proper use of grenades

WARGEAR
GRENADES

Item	Price	Rarity
Blasting charges	35 credits	Rare (8)
Choke gas grenades	50 credits	Rare (9)
Demo charges	50 credits	Rare (12)
Frag grenades	30 credits	Common
Incendiary charges	40 credits	Rare (7)
Krak grenades	45 credits	Rare (8)
Melta bombs	60 credits	Rare (11)
Photon flash grenades	15 credits	Rare (9)
Scare gas grenades	45 credits	Rare (10)
Smoke grenades	15 credits	Common
Stun grenades	15 credits	Rare (8)

ARMOUR

Item	Price	Rarity
Carapace armour		
- light	80 credits	Rare (10)
- heavy	100 credits	Rare (11)
Flak armour	10 credits	Common
Hazard suit	10 credits	Rare (10)
Mesh armour	15 credits	Common

FIELD ARMOUR

Item	Price	Rarity
Conversion field	60 credits	Rare (11)
Displacer field	70 credits	Rare (12)
Refractor field	50 credits	Rare (10)

BIONICS

Item	Price	Rarity
Aortic superchargers – Mundane	65 credits	Rare (13)
Bionic eye – Mundane	45 credits	Rare (13)
Bionic arm – Mundane	45 credits	Rare (13)
Bionic leg – Mundane	25 credits	Rare (12)
Cortex cogitator – Mundane	15 credits	Rare (11)
Cortex cogitator – Improved	30 credits	Rare (12)
Lobo chip – Mundane	20 credits	Rare (11)
Lobo chip – Improved	45 credits	Rare (12)
Skeletal enhancers – Mundane	70 credits	Rare (13)

GANG EQUIPMENT

Item	Price	Rarity
Ammo cache	60 credits	Rare (8)
Booby traps		
- frag trap	20 credits	Common
- gas trap	40 credits	Rare (8)
- melta trap	50 credits	Rare (10)

'WHERE THE METAL MEETS THE MEAT!'

- Slogan for The Cyberbazar 'Odds and Arms', Sump Town

MITHRA THE SIBILANT
CHEAPSIDE SPEKTRES
HOUSE DELAQUE

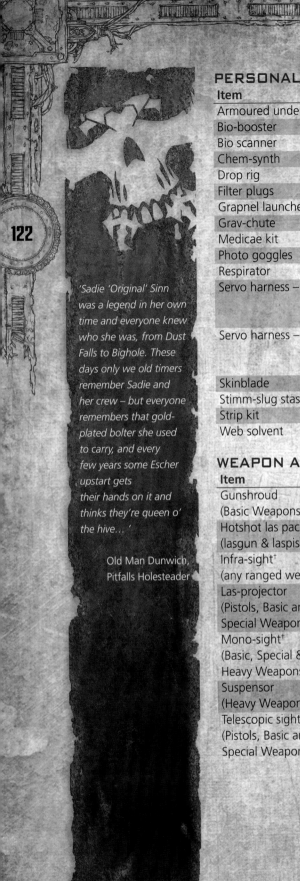

'Sadie 'Original' Sinn was a legend in her own time and everyone knew who she was, from Dust Falls to Bighole. These days only we old timers remember Sadie and her crew – but everyone remembers that gold-plated bolter she used to carry, and every few years some Escher upstart gets their hands on it and thinks they're queen o' the hive…'

Old Man Dunwich,
Pitfalls Holesteader

PERSONAL EQUIPMENT

Item	Price	Rarity
Armoured undersuit	25 credits	Rare (7)
Bio-booster	35 credits	Rare (8)
Bio scanner	30 credits	Rare (8)
Chem-synth	15 credits	Rare (12)
Drop rig	10 credits	Common
Filter plugs	10 credits	Common
Grapnel launcher	25 credits	Common
Grav-chute	50 credits	Rare (10)
Medicae kit	30 credits	Rare (9)
Photo goggles	35 credits	Rare (9)
Respirator	15 credits	Common
Servo harness – partial	130 credits	Rare (12) Rare (11 Goliath & Orlock) Rare (10 Van Saar)
Servo harness – full	160 credits	Rare (12) Rare (11 Goliath & Orlock) Rare (10 Van Saar)
Skinblade	10 credits	Common
Stimm-slug stash	30 credits	Rare (7)
Strip kit	15 credits	Common
Web solvent	25 credits	Rare (8)

WEAPON ACCESSORIES

Item	Price	Rarity
Gunshroud (Basic Weapons & Pistols)	20 credits	Rare (8)
Hotshot las pack (lasgun & laspistol only)	20 credits	Common
Infra-sight[†] (any ranged weapon)	40 credits	Rare (8)
Las-projector (Pistols, Basic and Special Weapons only)	35 credits	Rare (9)
Mono-sight[†] (Basic, Special & Heavy Weapons only)	35 credits	Rare (9)
Suspensor (Heavy Weapons only)	60 credits	Rare (10)
Telescopic sight[†] (Pistols, Basic and Special Weapons only)	25 credits	Common

STATUS ITEMS

Item	Price	Rarity
Extravagant Goods		
Exotic furs	50 credits	Rare (12)
Gold-plated gun	40 credits	Rare (10)
Master-crafted weapon	Cost of weapon +25%, rounded up to the nearest 5 credits	Rare (10)
Opulent jewellery	80 credits	Rare (11)
Uphive raiments	50 credits	Rare (10)
Servo-skulls		
Gun skull	65 credits	Rare (12)
Medi skull	80 credits	Rare (12)
Sensor skull	60 credits	Rare (12)

EXOTIC BEASTS

Item	Price	Rarity
Caryatid	*(see entry, page 114)	Rare (15)
Cephalopod Spekter	100 credits	Rare (11 Delaque only)
Cyberachnid	75 credits	Rare (10 Van Saar only)
Cyber-mastiff	100 credits	Rare (10 Orlock only)
Phyrr Cat	120 credits	Rare (12 Escher only)
Sheen bird	90 credits	Rare (12 Cawdor only)
Sumpkroc	130 credits	Rare (11 Goliath only)

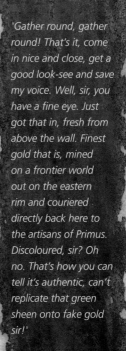

'Gather round, gather round! That's it, come in nice and close, get a good look-see and save my voice. Well, sir, you have a fine eye. Just got that in, fresh from above the wall. Finest gold that is, mined on a frontier world out on the eastern rim and couriered directly back here to the artisans of Primus. Discoloured, sir? Oh no. That's how you can tell it's authentic, can't replicate that green sheen onto fake gold sir!'

Dirk Canter,
Underhive Peddlar

WEAPON REFERENCE CHART

This reference section contains rules for all of the weapons and Wargear available to gangs and fighters through the Trading Post and House Equipment Lists.

This section also includes a full list of Wargear rules and Weapon Traits.

BASIC WEAPONS

Weapon	Rng S	Rng L	Acc S	Acc L	S	AP	D	Am	Traits
Autogun	8"	24"	+1	-	3	-	1	4+	Rapid Fire (1)
Reclaimed autogun	8"	24"	+1	-	3	-	1	5+	Rapid Fire (1)
Boltgun	12"	24"	+1	-	4	-1	2	6+	Rapid Fire (1)
Combat shotgun									
- salvo	4"	12"	+1	-	4	-	2	4+	Knockback, Rapid Fire (1)
- shredder ammo	-	T	-	-	2	-	1	4+	Scattershot, Template
- firestorm ammo	-	T	-	-	5	-1	1	6+	Blaze, Limited, Template
Lasgun	18"	24"	+1	-	3	-	1	2+	Plentiful
Las carbine	10"	24"	+1	-	3	-	1	4+	Plentiful, Rapid Fire (1)
Cawdor Polearm with autogun									
Polearm	E	2"	-1	-	S+1	-	1	-	Melee, Unwieldy, Versatile
Autogun	8"	24"	+1	-	3	-	1	5+	Rapid Fire (1)
Cawdor Polearm with blunderbuss									
Polearm	E	2"	-1	-	S+1	-	1	-	Melee, Unwieldy, Versatile
Blunderbuss									
- grape shot	-	T	-	-	2	-	1	6+	Plentiful, Scattershot
- purgation shot	-	T	-	-	3	-	1	6+	Blaze, Scarce
- Emperor's Wrath rounds	8"	12"	-	-1	4	-1	2	4+	Knockback, Pulverise
Sawn-off shotgun	4"	8"	+2	-	3	-	1	6+	Plentiful, Scattershot
Shotgun									
- acid rounds	4"	8"	+1	-	3	-1	1	5+	Blaze, Scattershot
- solid ammo	8"	16"	+1	-	4	-	2	4+	Knockback
- scatter ammo	4"	8"	+2	-	2	-	1	4+	Scattershot
- executioner ammo	4"	16"	-1	+1	4	-2	2	6+	Knockback, Limited
- inferno ammo	4"	16"	+1	-	4	-	2	5+	Blaze, Limited
Stub cannon	9"	18"	-	-	5	-	1	3+	Knockback
Suppression laser									
- broad burst	4"	8"	+2	-	2	-	1	4+	Plentiful, Scattershot
- short burst	8"	16"	+1	-	4	-	2	4+	Knockback, Plentiful
Throwing knives	Sx2	Sx4	-	-1	-	-1	-	5+	Scarce, Silent, Toxin

PISTOLS

Weapon	Rng S	Rng L	Acc S	Acc L	S	AP	D	Am	Traits
Autopistol	4"	12"	+1	-	3	-	1	4+	Rapid Fire (1), Sidearm
Compact autopistol (gun skull)	4"	12"	+1	-	2	-	1	4+	Rapid Fire (1), Scarce
Reclaimed autopistol	4"	12"	+1	-	3	-	1	5+	Rapid Fire (1), Sidearm
Bolt pistol	6"	12"	+1	-	4	-1	2	6+	Sidearm
Combi-pistol									
Primary component:									
- autopistol	4"	12"	+1	-	3	-	1	4+	Combi, Rapid Fire (1), Sidearm
- bolt pistol	6"	12"	+1	-	4	-1	2	6+	Combi, Sidearm
- stub gun	6"	12"	+2	-	3	-	1	4+	Combi, Plentiful, Sidearm
Secondary component:									
- hand flamer	-	T	-	-	3	-	1	5+	Blaze, Combi, Template, Unstable
- plasma pistol	6"	12"	+2	-	5	-1	2	5+	Combi, Scarce, Sidearm
Flechette pistol									
- solid ammo	4"	12"	+1	-	3	-	1	4+	Rapid Fire (1), Sidearm, Silent
- fleshbane ammo	4"	12"	-	-	-	-	-	6+	Rapid Fire (1), Scarce, Sidearm, Silent, Toxin
Hand flamer	-	T	-	-	3	-	1	5+	Blaze, Template
Laspistol	8"	12"	+1	-	3	-	1	2+	Plentiful, Sidearm
Las sub-carbine	4"	12"	+1	-	3	-	1	4+	Plentiful, Rapid Fire (1), Sidearm
Needle pistol	4"	9"	+2	-	-	-1	-	6+	Scarce, Sidearm, Silent, Toxin
Plasma pistol									
- low	6"	12"	+2	-	5	-1	2	5+	Scarce, Sidearm
- maximal	6"	12"	+1	-	7	-2	3	5+	Scarce, Sidearm, Unstable
Stub gun	6"	12"	+2	-	3	-	1	4+	Plentiful, Sidearm
- with dumdum rounds	5"	10"	+1	-	4	-	1	4+	Limited, Sidearm
Web pistol	-	T	-	-	4	-	-	6+	Silent, Template, Web
Web projector (Van Saar Cyberachnid)	-	T	-	-	2	-	-	6+	Scarce, Template, Web

'STUD' BORKER
STEEL BRUTES
HOUSE GOLIATH

SPECIAL WEAPONS

Weapon	Rng S	Rng L	Acc S	Acc L	S	AP	D	Am	Traits
Chemical cloud breath weapon (Escher Khimerix)	6"	12"	+1	-	3	-1	1	-	Blast (3")
Combi-weapon									
Primary component:									
- bolter	12"	24"	+1	-	4	-1	2	6+	Combi, Rapid Fire (1)
- lasgun	18"	24"	+1	-	3	-	1	2+	Combi, Plentiful
- autogun	8"	24"	+1	-	3	-	1	4+	Combi, Rapid Fire (1)
Secondary component:									
- flamer	-	T	-	-	4	-1	1	5+	Blaze, Combi, Template, Unstable
- grenade launcher (frag)	6"	24"	-1	-	3	-	1	*	Blast (3"), Knockback, Single Shot
- melta	6"	12"	+1	-	8	-4	3	4+	Combi, Melta, Scarce
- needler	9"	18"	+1	-	-	-1	-	6+	Combi, Scarce, Silent, Toxin
- plasma gun	12"	24"	+2	-	5	-1	2	5+	Combi, Rapid Fire (1), Scarce
Flamer	-	T	-	-	4	-1	1	5+	Blaze, Template
Gaseous eruption breath weapon (Escher Khimerix)	-	T	-	-	-	-	-	-	Gas, Template
Grav gun	9"	18"	+1	-	*	-1	2	5+	Blast (3"), Concussion, Graviton Pulse
Grenade launcher									
- frag grenades	6"	24"	-1	-	3	-	1	6+	Blast (3"), Knockback
- krak grenades	6"	24"	-1	-	6	-2	2	6+	-
- choke gas grenades	6"	24"	-1	-	-	-	-	5+	Blast (3"), Gas, Limited
- photon flash grenades	6"	24"	-	-	-	-	-	5+	Blast (5"), Flash
- scare gas grenades	6"	24"	-1	-	-	-	-	6+	Blast (3"), Fear, Gas, Limited
- smoke grenades	6"	24"	-1	-	-	-	-	4+	Smoke
Long las	18"	36"	-	+1	4	-	1	2+	Plentiful
Long rifle	24"	48"	-	+1	4	-1	1	4+	Knockback
Meltagun	6"	12"	+1	-	8	-4	3	4+	Melta, Scarce
Needle rifle	9"	18"	+2	-	-	-2	-	6+	Scarce, Silent, Toxin
'Nightshade' chem-thrower	-	T	-	-	-	-	-	5+	Gas, Silent, Template
Plasma gun									
- low	12"	24"	+2	-	5	-1	2	5+	Rapid Fire (1), Scarce
- maximal	12"	24"	+1	-	7	-2	3	5+	Scarce, Unstable
Rad gun	-	T	-	-	2	-2	1	4+	Rad-phage, Template
Web gun	-	T	-	-	5	-	-	5+	Silent, Template, Web

HEAVY WEAPONS

Weapon	Rng S	Rng L	Acc S	Acc L	S	AP	D	Am	Traits
Cawdor heavy crossbow									
- frag	15"	30"	-	-1	4	-	1	4+	Blast (5"), Knockback, Unwieldy
- krak	15"	30"	-	-1	6	-2	2	6+	Unwieldy
Harpoon launcher	6"	18"	+2	-	5	-3	1	5+	Drag, Impale, Scarce
Heavy bolter	18"	36"	+1	-	5	-2	2	6+	Rapid Fire (2), Unwieldy
Heavy flamer	-	T	-	-	5	-2	1	5+	Blaze, Template, Unwieldy
Heavy stubber	20"	40"	-	-1	4	-1	1	4+	Rapid Fire (2), Unwieldy
'Krumper' rivet cannon									
- rapid fire	3"	9"	+2	-	4	-1	2	3+	Rapid Fire (1), Rending
- super-heated	3"	9"	+2	-	6	-2	2	3+	Blaze, Rending
Lascannon	24"	48"	-	+1	10	-3	3	4+	Knockback, Unwieldy
Mining laser	18"	24"	-	-1	9	-3	3	3+	Unwieldy
Missile launcher									
- frag missile	24"	48"	+1	-	4	-1	1	6+	Blast (5"), Knockback, Unwieldy
- krak missile	24"	48"	+1	-	6	-2	3	6+	Unwieldy
Multi-melta	12"	24"	+1	-	8	-4	3	4+	Blast (3"), Melta, Scarce, Unwieldy
Plasma cannon									
- low	18"	36"	+1	-	6	-1	2	5+	Rapid Fire (1), Scarce, Unwieldy
- maximal	18"	36"	+1	-	8	-2	3	5+	Blast (3"), Scarce, Unstable, Unwieldy
Rad cannon	16"	32"	-	-1	2	-2	1	4+	Blast (5"), Rad-phage, Unwieldy
Seismic cannon									
- short wave	12"	24"	-	-1	6	-1	2	5+	Knockback, Rapid Fire (1), Seismic, Unwieldy
- long wave	12"	24"	-1	-	3	-	1	5+	Knockback, Rapid Fire (2), Seismic, Unwieldy
Twin-linked heavy las carbine (Van Saar Arachni-rig)	15"	30"	+1	-	4	-	1	4+	Plentiful, Rapid Fire (3)
Twin-linked heavy stubber (Cawdor Stig-Shambler)	20"	40"	-	-1	4	-1	2	4+	Rapid Fire (3), Unwieldy

GRENADES

Weapon	Rng S	Rng L	Acc S	Acc L	S	AP	D	Am	Traits
Blasting charges	-	Sx2	-	-	5	-1	2	5+	Blast (5"), Grenade, Knockback
Choke gas grenades	-	Sx3	-	-	-	-	-	5+	Blast (3"), Gas, Grenade
Demo charges	-	Sx2	-	-	6	-3	3	*	Blast (5"), Grenade, Single Shot
Frag grenades	-	Sx3	-	-	3	-	1	4+	Blast (3"), Grenade, Knockback
Incendiary charges	-	Sx3	-	-	3	-	1	5+	Blast (5"), Blaze, Grenade
Krak grenades	-	Sx3	-	-1	6	-2	2	4+	Demolitions, Grenade
Melta bombs	-	Sx3	-	-1	8	-4	3	6+	Demolitions, Grenade, Melta, Scarce
Photon flash grenades	-	Sx3	-	-	-	-	-	5+	Blast (5"), Flash, Grenade
Rad grenades	-	Sx3	-	-	2	-2	1	4+	Blast (3"), Grenade, Rad-phage
Scare gas grenades	-	Sx3	-	-	-	-	-	6+	Blast (3"), Fear, Gas, Grenade
Smoke grenades	-	Sx3	-	-	-	-	-	4+	Grenade, Smoke
Stun grenades	-	Sx3	-	-	2	-1	1	4+	Concussion, Grenade

BOOBY TRAPS

Weapon	Rng S	Rng L	Acc S	Acc L	S	AP	D	Am	Traits
Frag trap	-	-	-	-	3	-	1	-	Blast (5"), Knockback, Single Shot
Gas trap	-	-	-	-	-	-	-	-	Blast (5"), Gas, Single Shot
Melta trap	-	-	-	-	8	-4	3	-	Blast (5"), Melta, Single Shot

CLOSE COMBAT WEAPONS

Weapon	Rng S	Rng L	Acc S	Acc L	S	AP	D	Am	Traits
Knives									
Fighting knife	-	E	-	-	S	-1	1	-	Backstab, Melee
Power knife	-	E	-	-	S+1	-2	1	-	Backstab, Melee, Power
Stiletto knife	-	E	-	-	-	-	-	-	Melee, Toxin
Close Combat Weapons									
Arc welder ('Jotunn' Servitor)	-	E	-	-	S+2	-3	3	-	Blaze, Melee
Augmetic fist ('Jotunn' Servitor)	-	E	-	-	S+1	-1	2	-	Knockback, Melee
Axe	-	E	-	-	S+1	-	1	-	Disarm, Melee
Beak & talons (Cawdor Sheen bird)	-	E	-	-	S	-1	2	-	Melee, Rending
Brute cleaver	-	E	-	-	S	-1	1	-	Disarm, Melee
Cawdor polearm (Cawdor Stig-shambler)	E	2"	-1	-	S+1	-	1	-	Melee, Unwieldy, Versatile
Chainaxe	-	E	-	+1	S+1	-1	1	-	Disarm, Melee, Parry, Rending
Chainsword	-	E	-	+1	S	-1	1	-	Melee, Parry, Rending
Digi laser	E	3"	-	-	1	-	1	6+	Digi, Melee, Versatile
Ferocious jaws (Goliath Sumpkroc)	-	E	-	-	S	-1	1	-	Melee, Rending
Flail	-	E	-	+1	S+1	-	1	-	Entangle, Melee
Grav-fist (Ambot)									
- melee	-	E	-	-	S	-1	2	-	Melee, Pulverise
- ranged	6"	12"	+1	-	*	-1	2	5+	Blast (3"), Graviton Pulse, Concussion
Heavy club (Cawdor Stig-shambler)	-	E	-	-	S	-	2	-	Melee
Maul (club)	-	E	-	-	S	+1	2	-	Melee
Mutated fists & bone Spurs (Goliath 'Zerker)	E	2"	-	-	S+1	-2	2	-	Knockback, Melee, Pulverise, Versatile
Open fists (Goliath 'Zerker)	-	E	-	-	S	-1	1	-	Knockback, Melee
Razor Sharp Talons (Escher Khimerix)	-	E	-	-	S+1	-2	3	-	Melee, Rending
Savage Bite (Cyber-mastiff)	-	E	-	-	S	-2	1	-	Disarm, Melee
Servo arm (Van Saar Servo-suit)	E	3"	-	+1	S	-	1	-	Melee, Versatile
Servo claw	-	E	-	-	S+2	-	2	-	Melee
Servitor combat weapon (Orlock Lugger)	-	E	-	-	S	-1	1	-	Knockback, Melee
Spud-jacker	-	E	-	-	S+1	-	1	-	Knockback, Melee
Stiletto sword	-	E	-	-	-	-1	-	-	Melee, Parry, Toxin
Sword	-	E	-	+1	S	-1	1	-	Melee, Parry
Talons (Escher Khimerix and Phyrr Cat)	-	E	-	-	S	-1	2	-	Melee, Pulverise
Tunnelling claw (Ambot)									
- melee	-	E	-	-	S	-1	2	-	Melee
- ranged	4"	8"	-	-	6	-2	2	5+	Melta, Scarce, Sidearm
Venomous bite (Van Saar Cyberachnid)	-	E	-	-	-	-	-	-	Melee, Toxin
Web gauntlet	-	E	-	+1	3	-	-	-	Backstab, Melee, Web

128

Weapon	Rng S	Rng L	Acc S	Acc L	S	AP	D	Am	Traits
Power/Shock weapons									
'Hystrar' pattern energy shield	-	E	-	-	S	-	1	-	Energy Shield, Knockback, Melee
Las cutter	E	2"	+1	-	9	-3	2	6+	Melee, Scarce, Versatile
Power sword	-	E	-	-	S+1	-2	1	-	Melee, Parry, Power
Power axe	-	E	-	-	S+2	-2	1	-	Disarm, Melee, Power
Power hammer	-	E	-	-	S+1	-1	2	-	Melee, Power
Power pick	-	E	-	-	S+1	-3	1	-	Melee, Power, Pulverise
Power maul	-	E	-	-	S+2	-1	1	-	Melee, Power
Shock baton	-	E	-	-	S	-	1	-	Melee, Parry, Shock
Shock stave	E	2"	-	-	S+1	-	1	-	Melee, Shock, Versatile
Shock tendrils (Delaque Cephalopod Spekter)	E	2"	-	-	S+1	-	1	-	Melee, Shock, Versatile
Shock whip	E	3"	-1	-	S+1	-	1	-	Melee, Shock, Versatile
Thunder hammer	-	E	-	-	S+1	-1	3	-	Melee, Power, Shock
Two-Handed Weapons									
Chain glaive	E	2"	-1	-	S+2	-2	2	-	Melee, Unwieldy, Versatile
Heavy rock cutter	-	E	-	-	S+4	-4	3	-	Melee, Unwieldy
Heavy rock drill	-	E	-	-	S+2	-3	2	-	Melee, Pulverise, Unwieldy
Heavy rock saw	-	E	-	+1	S+3	-3	2	-	Melee, Rending, Unwieldy
'Renderizer' serrated axe	-	E	-	-	S+2	-1	2	-	Melee, Pulverise, Unwieldy
Two-handed axe	-	E	-	-1	S+2	-	2	-	Melee, Unwieldy
Two-handed hammer	-	E	-	-1	S+1	-	3	-	Knockback, Melee, Unwieldy

ONIA LARZ
COLDFIRE CABAL
HOUSE VAN SAAR

ARMOUR

A fighter may only be equipped with one type of armour at a time.

ARMOURED BODYGLOVE

Van Saar fighters are somewhat protected from the effects of their own rad weapons by their armour and are therefore immune to the effects of the Rad-phage Weapon Trait (i.e., they will not suffer the additional Flesh Wound) unless otherwise noted. If a fighter is wearing an armoured bodyglove, their save roll is improved by 1. For example, if they are wearing flak armour and an armoured bodyglove, they would have a 5+ save, which would be increased to 4+ against Blasts. If a fighter does not already have a save roll, an armoured bodyglove grants a 6+ save. An armoured bodyglove may be combined with other types of armour. It may not, however, be combined with an armoured undersuit.

CARAPACE

Light: Light carapace armour grants a 4+ save roll.

Heavy: Heavy carapace armour grants a 4+ save roll. This is increased to 3+ against attacks originating within the fighter's vision arc (the 90° arc to their front); check this before the fighter model is placed Prone and is Pinned. If it is not clear if the attacker is within the fighter's front arc, use a Vision Arc template to check – if the centre of the attacker's base is within the arc, use the 3+ save roll. Against attacks with the Blast trait, use the centre of the Blast marker in place of the attacker. If the fighter does not have a facing (for example, if they are prone), use the 4+ save roll. However, due to the extra weight of this armour, the fighter's Initiative is reduced by -1 and their movement by 1" when making a Charge action.

FLAK

Flak armour grants a 6+ save roll. Against weapons that use a Blast marker or Flame template, this is increased to a 5+ save roll.

FURNACE PLATES

Furnace plates grant a 6+ save roll. This is increased to a 5+ save roll against attacks originating within the fighter's vision arc (the 90° arc to their front); check this before the fighter model is placed Prone and is Pinned. If it is not clear if the attacker is within the fighter's front arc, use a Vision Arc template to check – if the centre of the attacker's base is within the arc, use the 5+ save roll. Against attacks with the Blast trait, use the centre of the Blast marker in place of the attacker. If the fighter does not have a facing (for example, if they are Prone) use the 6+ save roll.

HAZARD SUIT

The Ash Wastes are a hostile place, their dunes are frequently toxic or corrosive, and strong winds whip up regular ash storms capable of blasting any exposed skin raw in minutes. Consequently, those such as ash crust miners and the poor wretches who maintain a hive's outer armoured skin frequently wear heavy suits of rubberised canvas with vulcanised plates that protect them from the dangers of their working environment. A hazard suit grants a 6+ save roll. Additionally, when a hazard suit is combined with a respirator, the fighter's Toughness is increased by 3 against Gas attacks, rather than the usual 2. Finally, a fighter wearing a hazard suit is immune to the Blaze and Rad-phage traits.

MESH

Mesh armour grants a 5+ save roll.

FIELD ARMOUR

Any fighter may wear a force field. These provide an alternative to conventional armour and may be worn as well as conventional armour. The save they offer cannot be modified by a weapon's Armour Piercing value. However, a fighter can only make one save attempt per attack, therefore you must choose to either make a save attempt using the fighter's armour save, or using a field.

CONVERSION FIELD

A conversion field works by transforming the kinetic energy of an attack into light energy, absorbing the impact in a blinding flash. When a fighter wearing a conversion field is hit by an attack, roll a D6. On a 5+, the conversion field works and the attack has no further effect. However, any fighters, friend or foe, within 3" of the wearer count as being hit by a weapon with the Flash trait as the field reacts in a tremendous burst of light. Note that the wearer is unaffected by this flash of light as they are inside the field.

DISPLACER FIELD

A displacer field reacts to the energy of an impact by teleporting the wearer a safe distance away. The harder the impact, the further the wearer will be moved. If a fighter wearing a displacer field is hit, roll a D6. On a 4+, the fighter is moved a number of inches equal to the Strength of the attack in a random direction, determined by rolling a Scatter dice, and the hit is ignored (even if any part of the fighter is still under the Template – if the attack used one – after

being displaced). A displacer field will not deposit its wearer inside a terrain feature – the fighter will move by the shortest route possible so that it can be placed clear of any impassable terrain features. Similarly, the fighter's base cannot overlap another fighter's base and the wearer must be moved by the shortest route possible until its base can be placed without overlapping. Note that the wearer may not end up within 1" of an enemy fighter as a result of being displaced and must be moved by the shortest possible route so that they can be placed 1" away.

However, displacer fields are notoriously oblivious to safe footings. In a Zone Mortalis game, a fighter wearing a displacer field may be deposited above a pit fall or similar hazard. In a Sector Mechanicus game, a fighter above ground level may simply be flung into the open air. If any part of the fighter's base ends overhanging a hazard or overhanging a platform edge, the fighter must pass an Initiative test or will fall, following all of the rules for falling as required by the terrain type being fought over. If the entirety of the fighter's base is over a hazard or in the open air, they will simply fall.

If a fighter wearing a displacer field is transported off the board, they immediately go Out of Action.

If an attack does not have a Strength value, then a displacer field cannot work against it.

REFRACTOR FIELD

A refractor field bends the energy of an attack around the wearer, harmlessly distributing it over a large area and robbing the attack of its lethal force. When a fighter wearing a refractor field is hit by an attack, roll a D6. On a 5+, the hit is ignored.

However, should the field work and the hit be ignored, roll another D6. If the result is a 1, then the field has been overburdened by the attack and its generator is burned out. Remove the refractor field from the fighter's card, it no longer works.

BIONICS

Bionics are a way to repair damage sustained by fighters as a result of violence and hardship. Not only can Lasting Injuries be negated through the vigorous application of bionics, but the chances of suffering similar injuries in the future can be greatly reduced.

MUNDANE BIONICS

Should a fighter suffer any Lasting Injury as a result of going Out of Action which permanently reduces one or more of their characteristics, the injured body part may be replaced with a bionic prosthesis, thus restoring some degree of lost function. The price of getting a Doc to install the bionic is included in its cost. All Mundane bionics will increase one of the characteristics listed in their description by +1, thus negating part or all of the effect of the Lasting Injury.

MULTIPLE CHARACTERISTICS: Players should note that some Lasting Injuries only cause one characteristic to be decreased whilst other Lasting Injuries cause two characteristics to be decreased. Where a Lasting Injury causes two characteristics to be decreased, the bionic will give a choice of which characteristic is improved. If a fighter wishes to rectify two characteristic decreases caused by a Lasting Injury, they should look at purchasing an Improved bionic (as follows). They cannot purchase two Mundane bionics in order to rectify the effects of a single Lasting Injury.

IMPROVED BIONICS

As with Mundane bionics, any fighter that has suffered a Lasting Injury as a result of going Out of Action which permanently reduces two of their characteristics may replace the injured body part with Improved bionics. Improved bionics may be bought from the Trading Post in the same way as other items, provided that their Availability level has been met. The price of getting a Doc to install the bionic is included in its cost. All Improved bionics exist to allow a fighter that has suffered a Lasting Injury that decreases two characteristics to increase both at the same time, for a higher cost. Consequently, Lasting Injuries that only cause one characteristic to be decreased do not have the Improved bionics option.

CHARACTERISTIC INCREASES AND BIONICS: If a characteristic has been increased since the injury was sustained as a result of any Advancements, any bionics purchased (Mundane and Improved), may still increase the characteristic by 1 but may not take any characteristics beyond the maximum characteristics.

BIONICS AND RECOVERY: If a fighter is In Recovery when bionics are purchased, they will remain In Recovery as described in the campaign rules. Purchasing bionics does not negate the need to recover from an injury, even if the bionics mitigate the long-term effects.

DAMAGED BIONICS

When a fighter takes a fresh Lasting Injury to a location previously injured and subsequently replaced with bionics, there is a chance that their bionics will save them from further harm, taking only minor damage that can easily be repaired. Roll a D6. On a 1-3, the Lasting Injury is applied as normal (perhaps a fighter with a bionic left leg has sustained a similar injury to their right leg, for example). On a 4+, the bionics are hit and the effects of the Lasting Injury are ignored. However, if hit, there is a chance that the bionics will be irreparably damaged. Roll a D6. On a 2+, the bionics are scratched and dented but suffer no long-term effects. On a 1, however, the bionics are damaged beyond repair, the effects of the Lasting Injury are applied and the previous benefits of the bionics are lost, meaning that any characteristic increases granted by the bionics are also lost.

'GHAST'
THE ASH WALKERS
HOUSE DELAQUE

132

LOBO CHIP (HUMILIATED LASTING INJURY TABLE RESULT)

The underhive is dangerous and more than enough to break the mind of a ganger. Some fighters choose to get a lobo chip hammered into their cranium, diminishing their emotions to a dull murmur.

MUNDANE – Increase *either* the fighter's Leadership or Cool by +1.

IMPROVED – Increase *both* the fighter's Leadership and Cool by +1.

CORTEX-COGITATOR (HEAD INJURIES LASTING INJURY TABLE RESULT)

A spinal thought-shunt, the cortex-cogitator enhances or repairs a fighter's reasoning processes and mental fortitude.

MUNDANE – Increase *either* the fighter's Intelligence or Willpower by +1.

IMPROVED – Increase *both* the fighter's Intelligence and Willpower by +1.

BIONIC EYE (EYE INJURIES LASTING INJURY TABLE RESULT)

From bespoke models crafted to match a user's own natural organs, to crude hatchet jobs prised from the ocular sockets of smashed servo-skulls, bionic eyes restore sight.

MUNDANE – The fighter's Ballistic Skill is increased by +1.

BIONIC ARM (HAND INJURIES LASTING INJURY TABLE RESULT)

A good bionic arm is another weapon in its user's arsenal, able to both replace the function of an arm but also act as a handy club.

MUNDANE – The fighter's Weapon Skill is increased by +1.

BIONIC LEG (HOBBLED LASTING INJURY TABLE RESULT)

At its most basic, a bionic leg replaces the function of a flesh and blood limb, whether cobbled together from old servitor bits or crafted from advanced materials.

MUNDANE – The fighter's Movement is increased by +1".

SKELETAL ENHANCERS (SPINAL INJURY LASTING INJURY TABLE RESULT)

Skeletal enhancers repair damage and function to a fighter's strength, hardening bone and muscle with servo-assisted overlays or hydraulic body-rigs.

MUNDANE – The fighter's Strength is increased by +1.

AORTIC SUPERCHARGER (ENFEEBLED LASTING INJURY TABLE RESULT)

An aortic supercharger increases heart and organ function, granting a fighter exceptional stamina and the ability to shrug off injury.

MUNDANE – The fighter's Toughness is increased by +1.

EQUIPMENT

This section covers equipment carried by fighters and used by gangs to help them survive the rigours of battle and the harsh environment of the underhive.

AMMO CACHE

Ammo caches are added to the gang's Stash, instead of being carried by a particular fighter. Immediately after the last of the fighters in the crew is set up at the start of a battle, the controlling player can choose to set up any ammo caches from their Stash. If the scenario has an attacker and a defender, and this gang is defending, roll a D6 for each of their ammo caches. On a 1-4, they were not expecting the attackers and the caches cannot be used. On a 5 or 6, they are lucky enough to have them to hand. Each ammo cache must be set up within 1" of one of their fighters, and within their deployment zone if the scenario has one. It is then deleted from the gang's Stash. During the battle, ammo caches follow the rules on page 122 of the *Necromunda Rulebook*.

ARMOURED UNDERSUIT

An armoured undersuit may be worn in addition to any armour type, with the exception of an armoured bodyglove. If a fighter is wearing an armoured undersuit, their save roll is improved by 1. For example, if they are wearing flak armour and an armoured undersuit, they would have a 5+ save, which would be increased to 4+ against Blasts. If a fighter does not already have a save roll, an armoured undersuit grants a 6+ save.

BIO-BOOSTER

The first time in each game that an Injury roll is made for a fighter with a bio-booster, one less Injury dice is rolled. If only one dice was being rolled, two dice are rolled and the player controlling the fighter with the bio-booster can discard one of them.

BIO-SCANNER

If a fighter with a bio-scanner is a sentry in a scenario that uses the Sentries special rule, they can attempt to spot attackers even if they are not within their vision arc. In addition, the D6 roll to see whether a fighter is spotted has a +1 modifier (a natural 1 still fails).

BOMB DELIVERY RATS

A fighter equipped with bomb delivery rats may deploy one per turn to carry a single grenade of a type that fighter is equipped with by performing a Prime Bomb Rat (Basic) action. When a bomb delivery rat is deployed, make an Ammo roll for the grenade used as if it had been used normally. The fighter may run out of grenades before they run out of rats!

When the bomb delivery rat is deployed, place it so that the edge of its base is touching that of the fighter and make an Intelligence check for the fighter. If the check is passed, the fighter may choose the direction in which the rat moves. If the check is failed, the rat will move in a direction determined by rolling a Scatter dice. In either case, the rat may move up to 6". Bomb delivery rats ignore all terrain when moving, except any that would normally be impassable, such as walls. They suffer no penalties for climbing, they will never fall, and they may freely leap any gap of 2" or less. Wider gaps are considered impassable.

A bomb delivery rat is not a fighter and may pass within 1" of other models. Should the rat end its movement within 1" of, or in base to base contact with, a fighter, friend or enemy, or another bomb delivery rat, roll a D6. On a 2+, the grenade will go off. On a 1, the grenade proves to be a dud and the rat vanishes into the darkness to dwell upon its good fortune. In either case, the rat is removed from play.

At the start of every subsequent round, after rolling for Priority but before activating any fighters, if the bomb delivery rat has not exploded then it will activate again. Check to see if it is within 9" of the fighter that deployed it. If it is, and if that fighter is Standing and Active or Prone and Pinned, make an Intelligence check for the fighter. If this is passed, the

rat will immediately move up to 6" in a direction of the controlling player's choosing. If it is beyond 9", the Intelligence check is failed, the fighter is Standing and Engaged or Prone and Seriously Injured or if the fighter has been taken Out of Action, then the rat will move 6" in a direction determined by rolling a Scatter dice. Should the rat end its movement within 1" of a fighter, friend or enemy, or another bomb delivery rat, roll a D6. On a 2+, the grenade will go off. On a 1, the grenade proves to be a dud. In either case, the rat is removed from play.

Any fighter may attempt to shoot at a bomb delivery rat or make a melee attack against one as if it were an enemy fighter. However, there is always an additional -1 modifier on any hit roll made against a bomb delivery rat. If the rat is hit, roll a D6. On a 4+, the grenade goes off. On a 1-3, the grenade does not go off. In either case, once a bomb delivery rat has been hit by a shooting or melee attack, it is removed from play.

BOOBY TRAPS – FRAG, GAS AND MELTA

A booby trap is represented by a marker placed upon the battlefield at the start of the game, after the battlefield has been set up but before deploying any fighters. If both gangs possess and wish to use booby traps, the defender or the winner of a roll-off (if there is no defender) places theirs first.

If any fighter, friendly or enemy, comes within 2" of a booby trap for any reason, they risk setting the booby trap off. Roll a D6. On a 1, the booby trap is a dud and is removed from the battlefield. On a 2 or 3, the booby trap does not go off but is left in place. On a 4, 5 or 6, the booby trap is triggered and will explode. The profiles for booby traps can be found on page 127. The movement of a moving fighter is interrupted whilst this roll is resolved. If the booby trap does not go off, their movement continues after the roll is made. If the booby trap does go off, and the fighter is Pinned or Injured as a result, their movement ends.

Any fighter can target a booby trap with ranged attacks. Doing so has a -1 modifier to the hit roll at Short range, or a -2 modifier at Long range. If the booby trap is hit, roll a D6. On a 1-2, it is unaffected. On a 3-4, it is immediately triggered. On a 5-6, it is disarmed and removed.

CHEM-SYNTH
At the start of their activation, a Standing and Active or Standing and Engaged fighter with a chem-synth can choose to make an Intelligence check. If the check is passed, any Gas or Toxin weapons they use until the end of their activation are enhanced and the target's Toughness is reduced by 1 when resolving those attacks.

CULT ICON
Only one fighter in a gang may carry a cult icon, this must be either the gang Leader or a Champion. This symbol of dedication and devotion serves to inspire gang members to greater acts in battle. When the Leader or Champion carrying the icon makes a group activation, they may activate one additional Readied fighter within 3", meaning that the Leader may activate three additional fighters whilst a Champion may activate two additional fighters.

DROP RIG
An Active fighter with a drop rig can make the following action while they are within 1" of the edge of a platform: Descend (Basic) – The fighter makes a move of up to 3" horizontally and up to 12" vertically. Any vertical movement must be downwards, i.e., towards the ground.

FILTER PLUGS
If a fighter with filter plugs is hit by a weapon with the Gas trait, their Toughness is increased by 1 for the purposes of the roll to see whether they are affected. Filter plugs are one use; if a fighter uses them during a battle, they are deleted from their Fighter card when the battle ends.

GRAPNEL LAUNCHER
An Active fighter with a grapnel launcher can make the following action: Grapnel (Double) – The fighter can move up to 12" in a straight line, in any direction. This move can take them to a different level, as long as they do not move through any terrain.

GRAV CHUTE
If the fighter falls or jumps down to a lower level, they do not suffer any damage – they simply move down without any rolls being made.

MEDICAE KIT
When a fighter with a medicae kit assists a friendly fighter's Recovery test, roll an extra Injury dice then choose one to discard.

PHOTO-GOGGLES

A fighter with photo-goggles can attack through smoke clouds, can make ranged attacks against fighters 12" away under the Pitch Black rules (see page 120 of the *Necromunda Rulebook*) and may gain other benefits in low light conditions, depending upon the scenario. In addition, if they are hit by a Flash weapon, add 1 to the result of the Initiative test to see whether they become subject to the Blind condition.

RESPIRATOR

When a fighter with a respirator is hit by a weapon with the Gas trait, their Toughness is increased by 2 for the purposes of the roll to see whether they are affected.

SERVO HARNESS – PARTIAL

A fighter wearing a partial servo harness gains a +2 modifier to their Strength characteristic and a +1 modifier to their Toughness characteristic. This may take them above their maximum characteristics but it is not a permanent increase and will be lost should the servo harness be lost or cease to function for any reason. Additionally, a fighter wearing a partial servo harness gains the benefits of suspensors on any Unwieldy ranged weapon they carry. However, a fighter wearing a partial servo harness reduces their Movement and Initiative by 1. This item cannot be combined with a servo claw or any other type of servo harness.

SERVO HARNESS – FULL

A fighter wearing a full servo harness gains all of the benefits of a partial servo harness, but without the negative modifiers to Movement and Initiative. This item cannot be combined with a servo claw or any other type of servo harness.

SKINBLADE

If the fighter is Captured at the end of a battle, they can attempt to escape. If they do, roll a D6. On a result of 1 or 2, they are unsuccessful. On a result of 3 or 4, they escape but are injured in the process – make a Lasting Injury roll for them. On a result of 5 or 6, they escape. A fighter who escapes is no longer Captured; however, their skinblade is lost and removed from their Fighter card.

STIMM-SLUG STASH

Once per game, a fighter with a stimm-slug stash can use it at the start of their turn, when they are chosen to make an action. Immediately discard one Flesh Wound from the fighter's card, if any are present. Until the end of the round, the fighter's Move, Strength and Toughness characteristics are each increased by 2. At the start of the End phase, roll a D6. On a 1, the stimm overload is too much – roll an Injury dice and apply the result to the fighter.

STRIP KIT

When a fighter with a strip kit makes an Intelligence check to operate a door terminal or bypass the lock on a loot casket, add 2 to the result.

WEB SOLVENT

When a fighter equipped with web solvent makes a Recovery check due to the Webbed condition (see page 144), roll an extra Injury dice, picking one of the dice to resolve it and discarding the other. Additionally, when a fighter equipped with web solvent assists a fighter subject to the Webbed condition with a Recovery test, roll an extra two Injury dice and choose which one to apply.

WEAPON ACCESSORIES

Weapon accessories marked with a dagger (†) may not be combined together on the same weapon. If one such accessory is purchased for a weapon, another may not be added.

GUNSHROUD (BASIC WEAPONS AND PISTOLS)

A weapon fitted with a gunshroud gains the Silent trait.

HOTSHOT LAS PACK (LASGUN AND LASPISTOL ONLY)

At the expense of reliability, a lasgun or laspistol (not including las carbines, las sub-carbines or suppression lasers) can be fitted with a hotshot las pack, increasing its Strength to 4 and Armour Piercing to -1. However, the weapon loses the Plentiful trait and its Ammo value is reduced to 4+.

INFRA-SIGHT (PISTOLS, BASIC, SPECIAL AND HEAVY WEAPONS)†

Weapons with the Rapid Fire (X) or Blast (3"/5") trait cannot be fitted with an infra-sight. A weapon with an infra-sight can be used to attack through smoke clouds (see page 144), and prove more effective in Pitch Black conditions (see page 120 of the *Necromunda Rulebook*). In addition, there is no hit modifier when the weapon targets a fighter in partial cover, and a -1 modifier (instead of -2) when it targets a fighter in full cover.

LAS-PROJECTOR (PISTOLS, BASIC AND SPECIAL WEAPONS)

The weapon's Short range accuracy bonus is improved by 1 (for example, if it is +1, it becomes +2; if it is -, it becomes +1; if it is -1, it becomes -).

MONO-SIGHT (BASIC, SPECIAL AND HEAVY WEAPONS)†

If the fighter attacks with this weapon after making an Aim action, add 2 to the result of the hit roll instead of 1.

SUSPENSORS (HEAVY WEAPONS)

An Unwieldy ranged weapon fitted with suspensors is far more manoeuvrable. Firing it becomes a Basic action rather than a Double action.

TELESCOPIC SIGHT (PISTOLS, BASIC AND SPECIAL WEAPONS)†

If a fighter attacks with this weapon after making an Aim action, the weapon's Short range accuracy modifier is used even if the target is within the weapon's Long range.

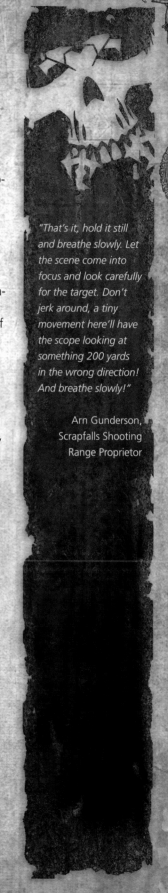

"That's it, hold it still and breathe slowly. Let the scene come into focus and look carefully for the target. Don't jerk around, a tiny movement here'll have the scope looking at something 200 yards in the wrong direction! And breathe slowly!"

Arn Gunderson,
Scrapfalls Shooting
Range Proprietor

STATUS ITEMS

Exotic Beasts, stolen relics or flamboyant opulence, when the money starts rolling in, underhive gangers are notorious for their tendency to flash their cash, spending it on all manner of extravagances that leave others in no doubt as to their success and importance, not only within their own gang, but within their House and the wider underhive. Unfortunately, such gaudy displays of wealth often leave others questioning the ganger's sense of style, and in extreme cases, their gullibility!

The following section covers the rules for Extravagant Goods and servo-skulls. The rules for Exotic Beasts can be found on page 104. These can be purchased for a Leader or Champions as normal when visiting the Trading Post in the post-battle sequence.

EXTRAVAGANT GOODS

Extravagant Goods are only available to Gang Leaders or Champions.

GOLD-PLATED GUN

Any weapon can be gold-plated. A fighter with a gold-plated gun adds +1 to their Leadership characteristic. Additionally, once per game, the fighter may re-roll a failed Ammo check.

EXOTIC FURS

Should this fighter make a Trade action in the post-battle sequence, they add an additional +1 modifier to the dice roll to determine the rarity of the items on offer.

MASTER-CRAFTED WEAPON

The fighter purchases a new weapon of exceptional craftsmanship. Any weapon may be master-crafted (note that grenades are Wargear, not weapons). The cost of a master-crafted weapon is that of the weapon plus 25%, with fractions rounded up to the nearest 5 credits. For example, a master-crafted bolter/plasma combi weapon would cost 145 credits (115 credits plus 25% equals 143.75 credits. Rounded up to the nearest 5 credits, this weapon costs 145 credits).

Note that the fighter may replace a weapon with which they are already equipped with a master-crafted version of that weapon, and that the original may be discarded and added to the gang's Stash. This is an exception to the norm.

A fighter may re-roll a single failed hit roll for this weapon every round.

OPULENT JEWELLERY

If this fighter makes a Medical Escort action in the post-battle sequence, they will attempt to impress the Doc with their visible wealth. Sometimes this works, sometimes it does not…

You may re-roll the dice when determining the fee the Doc charges, but you must accept the second result, even if it is worse.

UPHIVE RAIMENTS

If this fighter is not In Recovery during the post-battle sequence, their gang gains an extra D3x10 credits during the Collect Income step.

SERVO-SKULLS

Servo-skulls are only available to gang Leaders or Champions. All servo-skulls are treated as ordinary Wargear and should be recorded on their owner's Fighter card accordingly. Servo-skulls follow these rules:

- Servo-skulls must be represented by a separate model that must stay within 2" of the owning fighter. This is not a gang fighter or friendly model; it is purely a marker representing the servo-skull and matters only for its own line of sight and targeting purposes. Nor will they give away their owner's location, as they are assumed to be aware enough of stealthy movement to emulate it, and remain very low and close when needed.
- When the owner activates, the servo-skull will move with them. Servo-skulls ignore all terrain other than impassable terrain or walls, and can never fall.
- Servo-skulls cannot be targeted by shooting or melee attacks, and can never be Engaged in combat – they simply float away.
- Servo-skulls may be caught by a Blast marker or Flame template. If a servo-skull is caught under a Blast marker or Flame template, the attacker should roll a D6. On a 4-6, it is hit by the attack. On a 1-3, it is able to float clear of the area of the attack. Leave the model where it is and assume it has bobbed around to avoid the attack and returned to where it was. If a servo-skull is hit in this way, the owning player rolls a D6. On a 1, it is destroyed and should be removed from the owning fighter's Fighter card. On a 2-6, it is taken Out of Action and plays no further part in the game, but otherwise suffers no long-term effects.
- If the owning fighter leaves the table for any reason, the servo-skull will accompany them and takes no further part in the game.

SENSOR SKULL

A sensor skull grants the owning fighter the same benefits as a bio-scanner (see page 134). In addition, when the fighter takes an Aim action, they may add 2 to the result of any hit rolls they make for subsequent shots taken in the same activation rather than the usual 1. This bonus is in addition to any granted by any other wargear or skills the fighter may have.

MEDI SKULL

When making a Recovery test for the owning fighter, roll an extra Injury dice, then pick one of the dice to resolve and discard the other. This is in addition to any friendly fighters assisting the recovery and any other items such as medicae kits, so it is possible that the owning fighter may be rolling several Injury dice to choose from.

GUN SKULL

A gun skull is equipped with a compact autopistol (see page 125) and will target whatever or whoever the owning fighter does when they make a ranged attack. Simply roll one extra hit dice and one extra Ammo dice for the gun skull, ideally of a different colour to those being used for the fighter, to represent the gun skull making a ranged attack. Note though that range, line of sight and cover must be worked out from the gun skull itself rather than that of the owning fighter. If the owning fighter does not possess any ranged weapons, the gun skull may shoot at an enemy it can see, chosen by the owning fighter and following the normal target priority rules in relation to the owning fighter's position.

The owning fighter is never considered to be in the way of a gun skull's shooting attacks and cannot be hit by stray shots.

A gun skull has a BS of 5+, and may never benefit from aiming or any Wargear or skills that modify the owning fighter's to hit rolls.

WEAPON TRAITS

The following list contains all of the Weapon Traits in full.

BACKSTAB

If the attacker is not within the target's vision arc, add 1 to the attack's Strength.

BLAST (3"/5")

The weapon utilises a Blast marker, as described on page 65 of the *Necromunda Rulebook*.

BLAZE

After an attack with the Blaze trait has been resolved, roll a D6 if the target was hit but not taken Out Of Action. On a 4, 5 or 6, they become subject to the Blaze condition. When activated, a fighter subject to the Blaze condition suffers an immediate Strength 3, AP -1, Damage 1 hit before acting as follows:

- If Prone and Pinned the fighter immediately becomes Standing and Active and acts as described below.
- If Standing and Active the fighter moves 2D6" in a random direction, determined by the Scatter dice. The fighter will stop moving if this movement would bring them within 1" of an enemy fighter or into base contact with impassable terrain. If this movement brings them within ½" of the edge of a level or platform, they risk falling as described on page 63 of the *Necromunda Rulebook*. If this movement takes the fighter beyond the edge of a level or platform, they will simply fall. At the end of this move, the fighter may choose to become Prone and Pinned. The fighter may then attempt to put the fire out.
- If Standing and Engaged or Prone and Seriously Injured, the fighter does not move and attempts to put the fire out.

To attempt to put the fire out, roll a D6, adding 1 to the result for each other Active friendly fighter within 1". On a result of 6 or more, the flames go out and the Blaze marker is removed. Pinned or Seriously Injured fighters add 2 to the result of the roll to see if the flames go out.

COMBI

A combi-weapon has two profiles. When it is fired, pick one of the two profiles and use it for the attack. Due to the compact nature of the weapons, they often have less capacity for ammunition, and are prone to jamming and other minor issues. When making an Ammo check for either of the weapons, roll twice and apply the worst result. However, unlike most weapons that have two profiles, ammo for the two parts of the combi-weapon are tracked separately – if one profile runs Out of Ammo, the other can still fire unless it has also run Out of Ammo.

CONCUSSION

Any model hit by a Concussion weapon has their Initiative reduced by 2, to a minimum of 6+, until the end of the round.

DEMOLITIONS

Grenades with the Demolitions trait can be used when making close combat attacks against scenery targets (such as locked doors or scenario objectives). A fighter who uses a grenade in this way makes one attack (regardless of how many Attack dice they would normally roll), which hits automatically.

DIGI

A Digi weapon is worn mounted on a ring or hidden inside a glove. It can be used in addition to any other Melee weapon carried by the fighter, granting an additional close combat attack. A weapon with this trait does not count towards the maximum number of weapons a fighter can carry. However, the maximum number of weapons with this trait a fighter can carry is 10.

DISARM

If the hit roll for an attack made with a Disarm weapon is a natural 6, the target cannot use any weapons when making Reaction attacks for the remainder of that round – they make unarmed attacks instead.

DRAG

If a fighter is hit by a Drag weapon but not taken Out of Action, the attacker can attempt to drag the target closer after the attack has been resolved. If they do, roll a D6. If the score is equal to or higher than the target's Strength, the target is dragged D3" straight towards the attacker, stopping if they hit any terrain. If they move into another fighter (other than the attacker), both fighters are moved the remaining distance towards the attacker. If the weapon also has the Impale special rule and hits more than one fighter, only the last fighter to be hit can be dragged.

ENERGY SHIELD

An energy shield grants a +2 armour save modifier (to a maximum of 2+) against melee attacks that originate from within the fighter's vision arc (the 90° arc to their front), and a +1 armour save modifier against ranged attacks that originate from within the fighter's vision arc; check this before the fighter model is placed Prone and is Pinned. If it is not clear whether the attacker is within the target's front arc, use a Vision Arc template to check – if the centre of the attacker's base is within the arc, the energy shield can be used. Against attacks with the Blast trait, use the centre of the Blast marker in place of the attacker. If the target does not have a facing (for example, if they are Prone), the energy shield cannot be used.

ENTANGLE

Hits scored by weapons with the Entangle trait cannot be negated by the Parry trait. In addition, if the hit roll for an Entangle weapon is a natural 6, any Reaction attacks made by the target have an additional -2 hit modifier.

FEAR

If this attack would result in an Injury roll being made for any reason, no Injury roll is made and instead the opposing player makes a Nerve test for the target, subtracting 2 from the result. If the test fails, the target is immediately Broken and runs for cover.

FLASH

If a fighter is hit by a Flash weapon, no wound roll is made. Instead, make an Initiative check for the target. If it is failed, they become subject to the Blind condition. A Blind fighter loses their Ready marker; if they do not have a Ready marker, they do not gain a Ready marker at the start of the following round. Until the next time the fighter is activated, they cannot make any attacks other than Reaction attacks, for which any hit rolls will only succeed on a natural 6.

GAS

When a fighter is hit by an attack made by a Gas weapon, they are not Pinned and a wound roll is not made. Instead, roll a D6. If the result is equal to or higher than the target's Toughness, or is a natural 6, make an Injury roll for them (regardless of their Wounds characteristic). If the roll is lower than the target's Toughness, they shrug off the effects of the gas – no save roll can be made.

GRAVITON PULSE

Instead of rolling to wound normally with this weapon, any model caught in the Blast must instead roll equal to or under their Strength on a D6 (a roll of 6 always counts as a fail), or suffer Damage with no armour save roll allowed. After the weapon has been fired, leave the Blast marker in place. For the remainder of the round, any model moving through this area will use 2" of their Movement for every 1" they move. Remove the Blast marker during the End phase.

GRENADE

Despite being Wargear, grenades are treated as a special type of ranged weapon. A fighter equipped with grenades can throw one as a Shoot (Basic) action. Grenades do not have a Short range, and their Long range is determined by multiplying the fighter's Strength by the amount shown.

A fighter can only carry a limited number of grenades. The Firepower dice is not rolled when attacking with a grenade. Instead, after the attack has been resolved, an Ammo check is made automatically. If this is failed, grenades cannot be reloaded; the fighter has run out of that type of grenade and cannot use them for the remainder of the battle.

IMPALE

If an attack made by this weapon hits and wounds the target, and the save roll is unsuccessful (or no save roll is made), the projectile continues through them and might hit another fighter! Trace a straight line from the target, directly away from the attacker. If there are any fighters within 1" of this line, and within the weapon's Long range, the one that is closest to the target is at risk of being hit. Roll a D6. On a 3 or more, resolve the weapon's attack against that fighter, subtracting 1 from the Strength. The projectile can continue through multiple fighters in this way, but if the Strength is reduced to 0, it cannot hit any more fighters.

KNOCKBACK

If the hit roll for a weapon with the Knockback trait is equal to or higher than the target's Strength, they are immediately moved 1" directly away from the attacking fighter. If the fighter cannot be moved the full 1" because of impassable terrain or another fighter, they move as far as possible and the attack's Damage is increased by 1. If a Blast weapon has the Knockback trait, roll a D6 for each fighter that is hit. If the result is equal to or higher than their Strength, they are knocked back as described above – however, they are moved directly away from the centre of the Blast marker instead. If the centre of the Blast marker was over the centre of their base, roll a Scatter dice to determine which way they are moved. If a Melee weapon has the Knockback trait, the attacking fighter can choose to follow the target up, moving directly towards them after they have been knocked back to remain in base contact. If the attack was made across a barricade, the attacker cannot do this. If any part of the knocked back fighter's base crosses the edge of a platform, make an Initiative check. If this is failed, they will fall. If this is passed, they stop moving at the edge of the platform.

LIMITED

This special rule is applied to some special ammo types which can be purchased for weapons. If a weapon fails an Ammo check while using Limited ammo, they have run out – that ammo type is deleted from their Fighter card, and cannot be used again until more of that special ammo is purchased from the Trading Post. This is in addition to the normal rules for the weapon running Out of Ammo. The weapon can still be reloaded as normal, using its remaining profile(s).

MELEE

This weapon can be used during close combat attacks.

CYPHERED CTHEPA
THE ASH WALKERS
HOUSE DELAQUE

MELTA

If a Short range attack from a weapon with this Trait reduces a fighter to 0 wounds, no Injury dice are rolled – instead, any Injury dice that would be rolled cause an automatic Out of Action result.

PARRY

After an enemy makes close combat attacks against a fighter armed with a Parry weapon, the fighter can force the attacking player to re-roll one successful hit. If the fighter is armed with two Parry weapons, they can force the attacking player to re-roll two successful hits instead.

PLENTIFUL

Ammunition for this weapon is incredibly common. When reloading it, no Ammo check is required – it is automatically reloaded.

POWER

The weapon is surrounded by a crackling power field. Attacks made by Power weapons cannot be Parried except by other weapons with the Power trait. In addition, if the hit roll for a Power weapon is a natural 6, no save roll can be made against the attack (except Field armour save rolls) and its Damage is increased by 1.

PULVERISE

After making an Injury roll for an attack made by this weapon, the attacking player can roll a D6. If the result is equal to or higher than the target's Toughness, or is a natural 6, they can change one Injury dice from a Flesh Wound result to a Serious Injury result.

RAD-PHAGE

After fully resolving any successful hits a fighter suffers from a weapon with this Trait, roll an additional D6. If the roll is a 4 or higher, the fighter will suffer an additional Flesh Wound.

RAPID-FIRE (X)

When firing with a Rapid Fire weapon, a successful hit roll scores a number of hits equal to the number of bullet holes on the Firepower dice. In addition, the controlling player can roll more than one Firepower dice, up to the number shown in brackets (for example, when firing a Rapid Fire (2) weapon, up to two Firepower dice can be rolled). Make an Ammo check for each Ammo symbol that is rolled. If any of them fail, the gun runs Out of Ammo. If two or more of them fail, the gun has jammed and cannot be used for the rest of the battle.

If a Rapid Fire weapon scores more than one hit, the hits can be split between multiple targets. The first must be allocated to the original target, but the remainder can be allocated to other fighters within 3" of the first who are also within range and line of sight. These must not be any harder to hit than the original target – if a target in the open is hit, an obscured target cannot have hits allocated to it. Allocate all of the hits before making any wound rolls.

RENDING

If the roll to wound with a Rending weapon is a 6, then the attack causes 1 extra point of Damage.

SCARCE

Ammunition is hard to come by for Scarce weapons, and as such they cannot be reloaded – once they run Out of Ammo, they cannot be used again during the battle.

SCATTERSHOT

When a target is hit by a Scattershot attack, make D6 wound rolls instead of 1.

SEISMIC

If the target of a Seismic attack is Active, they are always Pinned – even if they have an ability that would normally allow them to avoid being Pinned by ranged attacks. In addition, if the wound roll for a Seismic weapon is a natural 6, no save roll can be made against that attack.

SHOCK

If the hit roll for a Shock weapon is a natural 6, the wound roll is considered to automatically succeed (no wound roll needs to be made).

SIDEARM

Weapons with this Trait can be used to make ranged attacks, and can also be used in close combat to make a single attack. Note that their Accuracy bonus only applies when making a ranged attack, not when used to make a close combat attack.

SILENT

In scenarios that use the Sneak Attack special rules, there is no test to see whether the alarm is raised when this weapon is fired. Additionally, if using the Pitch Black rules, a fighter using this weapon that is Hidden does not become Revealed.

SINGLE SHOT

This weapon can only be used once per game. After use, it counts as having automatically failed an Ammo check. There is no need to roll the Firepower dice unless the weapon also has the Rapid Fire (X) trait.

SMOKE

Smoke weapons do not cause hits on fighters – they do not cause Pinning, and cannot inflict wounds. Instead, mark the location where they hit with a counter. They generate an area of dense smoke, which extends 2.5" out from the centre of the counter, vertically as well as horizontally. Fighters can move through the smoke, but it blocks line of sight, so attacks cannot be made into, out of or through it. In the End phase, roll a D6. On a 4 or less, the cloud dissipates and the counter is removed.

TEMPLATE

Template weapons use the Flame template to determine how many targets they hit, as described on page 66 of the *Necromunda Rulebook*.

TOXIN

Instead of making a wound roll for a Toxin attack, roll a D6. If the result is equal to or higher than the target's Toughness, or is a natural 6, make an Injury roll for them (regardless of their Wounds characteristic). If the roll is lower than the target's Toughness, they shrug off the toxin's effects.

UNSTABLE

If the Ammo symbol is rolled on the Firepower dice when attacking with this weapon, there is a chance that the weapon will overheat in addition to needing an Ammo check. Roll a D6. On a 1, 2 or 3, the weapon suffers a catastrophic overload and the attacker is taken Out of Action. The attack is still resolved against the target.

UNWIELDY

A Shoot action made with this weapon counts as a Double action as opposed to a Single action. In addition, a fighter who uses a weapon with both the Unwieldy and Melee traits in close combat cannot use a second weapon at the same time – this one requires both hands to use.

VERSATILE

The wielder of a Versatile weapon does not need to be in base contact with an enemy fighter in order to Engage them in melee during their activation. They may Engage and make close combat attacks against an enemy fighter during their activation, so long as the distance between their base and that of the enemy fighter is equal to or less than the distance shown for the Versatile weapon's Long range characteristic. For example, a fighter armed with a Versatile weapon with a Long range of 2" may Engage an enemy fighter that is up to 2" away.

The enemy fighter is considered to be Engaged, but may not in turn be Engaging the fighter armed with the Versatile weapon unless they too are armed with a Versatile weapon, and so may not be able to make Reaction attacks.

At all other times other than during this fighter's activation, Versatile has no effect.

WEB

If the wound roll for a Web attack is successful, no wound is inflicted, and no save roll or Injury roll is made. Instead, the target automatically becomes Webbed. Treat the fighter as if they were Seriously Injured and roll for Recovery for them during the End phase (Web contains a powerful sedative capable of rendering the strongest fighter unconscious). If a Flesh Wound result is rolled during Recovery, apply the result to the fighter as usual and remove the Webbed condition. If a Serious Injury is rolled, the fighter remains Webbed. If an Out of Action result is rolled, the fighter succumbs to the powerful sedative and is removed from play, automatically suffering a result of 12-26 (Out Cold) on the Lasting Injuries table.

A fighter that is Webbed at the end of the game does not succumb to their Injuries and will automatically recover. However, during the Wrap Up, when rolling to determine if any enemy fighters are Captured at the end of the game, add +1 to the dice roll for each enemy fighter currently Webbed and include them among any eligible to be Captured.

SKILLS

This section presents the full list of all of the skills available to fighters. This section is split into eight lists, one for each skill set. Each entry lists the skill by name, and then its rules.

The following table summarises each of the skill sets, and can be used (by rolling a D6) to determine a random skill from one of the skill sets:

D6	Agility	Brawn	Combat	Cunning	Ferocity	Leadership	Shooting	Savant
1	Catfall	Bull Charge	Combat Master	Backstab	Berserker	Commanding Presence	Fast Shot	Ballistics Expert
2	Clamber	Bulging Biceps	Counter-attack	Escape Artist	Fearsome	Inspirational	Gunfighter	Connected
3	Dodge	Crushing Blow	Disarm	Evade	Impetuous	Iron Will	Hip Shooting	Fixer
4	Mighty Leap	Headbutt	Parry	Infiltrate	Nerves of Steel	Mentor	Marksman	Medicae
5	Spring Up	Hurl	Rain of Blows	Lie Low	True Grit	Overseer	Precision Shot	Munitioneer
6	Sprint	Iron Jaw	Step Aside	Overwatch	Unstoppable	Regroup	Trick Shot	Savvy Trader

CYCLELOS THREE EYE
SUMPTOWN WRAITHS
HOUSE DELAQUE

AGILITY

1. CATFALL
When this fighter falls or jumps down from a ledge, they count the vertical distance moved as being half of what it actually is, rounded up. In addition, if they are not Seriously Injured or taken Out of Action by a fall, make an Initiative test for them – if it is passed, they remain Standing rather than being Prone and Pinned.

2. CLAMBER
When this fighter climbs, the distance they move is not halved. In other words, they always count as climbing up or down a ladder.

3. DODGE
If this fighter suffers a wound from a ranged or close combat attack, roll a D6. On a 6, the attack is dodged and has no further effect; otherwise, continue to make a save or resolve the wound as normal.

If the model dodges a weapon that uses a Blast marker or Flame template, a roll of 6 does not automatically cancel the attack – instead, it allows the fighter to move up to 2" before seeing if they are hit. They cannot move within 1" of an enemy fighter.

4. MIGHTY LEAP
When measuring the distance of a gap this fighter wishes to leap across, ignore the first 2" of the distance. This means that a fighter with this skill may leap over gaps of 2" or less without testing against their Initiative. All other rules for leaping over gaps still apply.

5. SPRING UP
If this fighter is Pinned when they are activated, make an Initiative check for them. If the check is passed, the fighter may make a Stand Up (Basic) action for free. If the check is failed, the fighter may still stand up, but it costs one action, as usual.

6. SPRINT
If this fighter makes two Move (Simple) actions when activated during a round, they can use the second to Sprint. This lets them move at double their Movement characteristic for the second Move (Simple) action.

BRAWN

1. BULL CHARGE
When the fighter makes close combat attacks as part of a Charge (Double) action, any weapons with the Melee trait they use gain the Knockback trait and are resolved at +1 Strength.

2. BULGING BICEPS
This fighter may wield an Unwieldy weapon in one hand rather than the usual two. Note that Unwieldy weapons still take up the space of two weapons with regards to how many a fighter may carry.

3. CRUSHING BLOW
Before rolling to hit for the fighter's close combat attacks, the controlling player can nominate one dice to make a Crushing Blow. This cannot be a dice that is rolling for a weapon with the Pistol trait. If that dice hits, the attack's Strength and Damage are increased by one.

4. HEADBUTT
If the fighter is Standing and Engaged, they can make the following action:

HEADBUTT (BASIC) – Pick an Engaged enemy fighter and roll two D6. If either result is equal to or higher than their Toughness, they suffer a hit with a Strength equal to this fighter's +2, resolved at Damage 2. However, if both dice score lower than the enemy fighter's Toughness, this fighter instead suffers a hit equal to their own Strength, resolved at Damage 1.

5. HURL
If the fighter is Standing and Engaged, they can make the following action:

HURL (BASIC) – Pick an enemy fighter Engaged by, and in base contact with, this fighter or a Seriously Injured enemy fighter within 1" of this fighter. Make an Initiative check for the enemy fighter. If failed, the enemy fighter is hurled. Move the enemy fighter D3" in a direction of your choice – if they were Standing, they become Prone and Pinned after moving. If they come into base contact with a Standing fighter or any terrain, they stop moving and suffer a Strength 3, Damage 1 hit. If they come into base contact with another fighter, that fighter also suffers a Strength 3, Damage 1 hit, and becomes Prone and Pinned.

6. IRON JAW
This fighter's Toughness is treated as being two higher than normal when another fighter makes unarmed attacks against them in close combat.

COMBAT

1. COMBAT MASTER

The fighter never suffers penalties to their hit rolls for interference, and can always grant assists, regardless of how many enemy fighters they are Engaged with.

2. COUNTER-ATTACK

When this fighter makes Reaction attacks in close combat, they roll one additional Attack dice for each of the attacker's Attacks that failed to hit (whether they missed, were parried, etc).

3. DISARM

Any weapons with the Melee trait used by the fighter also gain the Disarm trait. If a weapon already has this Trait, then the target will be disarmed on a natural roll of a 5 or 6, rather than the usual 6.

4. PARRY

The fighter can parry attacks as though they were carrying a weapon with the Parry trait. If they already have one or more weapons with this Trait, they can parry one additional attack.

5. RAIN OF BLOWS

This fighter treats the Fight action as Fight (Simple) rather than Fight (Basic). In other words, this fighter may make two Fight (Simple) actions when activated.

6. STEP ASIDE

If the fighter is hit in close combat, the fighter can attempt to step aside. Make an Initiative check for them. If the check is passed, the attack misses. This skill can only be used once per enemy in each round of close combat – in other words, if an enemy makes more than one attack, the fighter can only attempt to step aside from one of them.

CUNNING

1. BACKSTAB

Any weapons used by this fighter with the Melee trait also gain the Backstab trait. If they already have this Trait, add 2 to the attack's Strength rather than the usual 1 when the Trait is used.

2. ESCAPE ARTIST

When this fighter makes a Retreat (Basic) action, add 2 to the result of their Initiative check (a natural 1 still fails). Additionally, if this fighter is Captured at the end of a battle, and if they are equipped with a skin blade, they may add 1 to the result of the dice roll to see if they can escape.

3. EVADE

If an enemy targets this fighter with a ranged attack, and this fighter is Standing and Active and not in partial cover or full cover, there is an additional -1 modifier to the hit roll, or a -2 modifier if the attack is at Long range.

4. INFILTRATE

If this fighter should be set up at the start of a battle, they may instead be placed to one side. Then, immediately before the start of the first round, their controlling player may set them up anywhere on the battlefield that is not visible to any enemy fighters, and not within 6" of any of them. If both players have fighters with this skill, take turns to set one up, starting with the winner of a roll-off.

5. LIE LOW

While this fighter is Prone, enemy fighters cannot target them with a ranged attack unless they are within the attacking weapon's Short range. Weapons that do not have a Short range are unaffected by this rule.

6. OVERWATCH

If this fighter is Standing and Active, and has a Ready marker on them, they can interrupt a visible enemy fighter's action as soon as it is declared but before it is carried out. This fighter loses their Ready marker, then immediately makes a Shoot (Basic) action, targeting the enemy fighter whose action they have interrupted. If the enemy is Pinned or Seriously Injured as a result, their activation ends immediately, and their action(s) are not made.

FEROCITY

1. BERSERKER

When this fighter makes close combat attacks as part of a Charge (Double) action, they roll one additional Attack dice.

2. FEARSOME

If an enemy wishes to make a Charge (Double) action that would result in them making one or more close combat attacks against this fighter, they must make a Willpower check before moving. If the check is failed, they cannot move and their activation ends immediately.

3. IMPETUOUS

When this fighter consolidates at the end of a close combat, they may move up to 4", rather than the usual 2".

4. NERVES OF STEEL

When the fighter is hit by a ranged attack, make a Cool check for them. If it is passed, they may choose not to be Pinned.

5. TRUE GRIT

When making an Injury roll for this fighter, roll one less Injury dice (for example, a Damage 2 weapon would roll one dice). Against attacks with Damage 1, roll two dice – the player controlling the fighter with True Grit can then choose one dice to discard before the effects of the other are resolved.

6. UNSTOPPABLE

Before making a Recovery check for this fighter in the End phase, roll a D6. If the result is 4 or more, one Flesh Wound they have suffered previously is discarded. If they do not have any Flesh Wounds, and the result is a 4 or more, roll one additional dice for the Recovery check and choose one to discard.

LEADERSHIP

1. COMMANDING PRESENCE

When this fighter activates to make a group activation, they may include one more fighter than normal as part of the group (i.e., a Champion could activate two other fighters instead of one, and a Leader could activate three).

2. INSPIRATIONAL

If a friendly fighter within 6" of this fighter fails a Cool check, make a Leadership check for this fighter. If the Leadership check is passed, then the Cool check also counts as having been passed.

3. IRON WILL

Subtract 1 from the result of any Bottle rolls whilst this fighter is on the battlefield and is not Seriously Injured.

4. MENTOR

Make a Leadership check for this fighter each time another friendly fighter within 6" gains a point of Experience. If the check is passed, the other fighter gains two Experience points instead of one.

5. OVERSEER

If the fighter is Standing and Active, they can attempt to make the following action:

ORDER (DOUBLE) – Pick a friendly fighter within 6". That fighter can immediately make two actions as though it were their turn to activate, even if they are not Ready. If they are Ready, these actions do not remove their Ready marker.

6. REGROUP

If this fighter is Standing and Active at the end of their activation, the controlling player may make a Leadership check for them. If this check is passed, each friendly fighter that is currently subject to the Broken condition and is within 6" immediately recovers from being Broken.

SHOOTING

1. FAST SHOT
This fighter treats the Shoot action as (Simple) rather than (Basic), as long as they do not attack with a weapon that has the Unwieldy trait (note that even if a skill or wargear item allows a fighter to ignore one aspect of the Unwieldy trait, Unwieldy weapons retain the Trait).

2. GUNFIGHTER
If this fighter uses the Twin Guns Blazing rule to attack with two weapons with the Sidearm trait, they do not suffer the -1 penalty to their hit rolls and can, if they wish, target a different enemy model with each weapon with the Sidearm trait.

3. HIP SHOOTING
If the fighter is Standing and Active, they can make the following action:

RUN AND GUN (DOUBLE) – The fighter may move up to double their Movement characteristic and then make an attack with a ranged weapon. The hit roll suffers an additional -1 modifier, and Unwieldy weapons can never be used in conjunction with this skill.

4. MARKSMAN
The fighter is not affected by the rules for Target Priority. In addition, if the hit roll for an attack made by the fighter with a ranged weapon (that does not have the Blast trait) is a natural 6, they score a critical hit and the weapon's Damage is doubled (if they are firing a weapon with the Rapid Fire trait, only the Damage of the first hit is doubled).

5. PRECISION SHOT
If the hit roll for a ranged attack made by this fighter is a natural 6 (when using a weapon that does not have the Blast trait), the shot hits an exposed area and no armour save can be made.

6. TRICK SHOT
When this fighter makes ranged attacks, they do not suffer a penalty for the target being Engaged or in partial cover. In addition, if the target is in full cover, they reduce the penalty to their hit roll to -1 rather than -2.

SAVANT

1. BALLISTICS EXPERT
When this fighter makes an Aim (Basic) action, make an Intelligence check for them. If the check is passed, they gain an additional +1 modifier to their hit roll.

2. CONNECTED
This fighter can make a Trade action during the post-battle sequence, in addition to any other actions they make (meaning they could even make two Trade actions). They cannot do this if they are unable to make actions during the post-battle sequence.

3. FIXER
In the Receive Rewards step of the post-battle sequence, as long as this fighter is not Captured or In Recovery, their gang earns an additional D3x10 credits. Note that they do not need to have taken part in the battle to gain this bonus.

4. MEDICAE
When this fighter assists a friendly fighter who is making a Recovery test, re-roll any Out of Action results. If the result of a re-rolled dice is also Out of Action, the result stands.

5. MUNITIONEER
Whenever an Ammo check is failed for this fighter, or another fighter from their gang within 6", it can be re-rolled.

6. SAVVY TRADER
When this fighter makes a Trade action in the post-battle sequence, add 1 to the result of the dice roll to determine the availability of Rare items on offer at the Trading Post on this visit. Additionally, the cost of one item may be reduced by 20 credits on this visit. Note that this means one item, not one type of Item. A single power sword may be purchased for 30 credits, but a second power sword will still cost 50 credits.

ROUND SEQUENCE

Each round is split into three phases, resolved one at a time:

1. PRIORITY PHASE

- **ROLL FOR PRIORITY:** Each player rolls a D6, the high roller takes priority. In the case of a tie, priority passes from the player that had priority in the previous round.
- **READY FIGHTERS:** Both players place a Ready marker on all of their fighters. Ready markers are removed after a fighter has been activated in the Action phase.

2. ACTION PHASE

- **FLEEING FIGHTERS:** If either gang has failed a Bottle test, make a Cool check for all of its fighters immediately before the controlling player picks their first fighter to activate. If any fail, they flee and are removed from the board. They take no further part in the battle. For the purposes of the scenario, they are considered to have been taken Out of Action.
- **ACTIVATE FIGHTERS:** Starting with the player with Priority, players take turns to pick one of their Ready fighters to activate. All fighters may perform two actions. Simple and Basic actions require one action to perform, Double actions require two actions to perform. Per activation, each Simple action may be performed twice, each Basic action may only be performed once. The actions available to a fighter may be limited depending upon their status (see Actions). Once a fighter has been activated, their Ready marker is removed.

3. END PHASE

- **BOTTLE TESTS:** If either or both player(s) has at least one fighter Seriously Injured or Out of Action, they roll a D6 and add the number of fighters in their crew that are Seriously Injured or Out of Action. If the result is higher than the total number of fighters in their starting crew, their remaining fighters bottle out. Once bottled out, fighters may flee the battlefield at the start of the Activation Phase.
- **RECOVERY TESTS:** For each Seriously Injured fighter on the battlefield, the controlling player rolls one (or more) Injury dice and applies the result.
- **RALLY TESTS:** Make a Cool check for each Broken fighter, adding 1 to the result for each friendly fighter that is not also Broken or Prone and Seriously Injured within 3". If the check is passed, the fighter is no longer Broken.

SHOOTING SEQUENCE

A fighter must target the closest eligible target when making a shooting attack. An enemy fighter is an eligible target if they are within the vision arc and line of sight of the attacker, even if they are Engaged by a friendly fighter. However, if the closest eligible target is Prone and Seriously Injured or harder to hit than one further away, the attacker may choose to ignore them. Otherwise, to attack an eligible target that is not the closest, the attacker must first pass a Cool check.

If attacking with any weapon with the Blast (X) trait, a fighter may target a point on the tabletop instead of an eligible enemy fighter. Shooting modifiers may apply as normal to this.

When any fighter makes an attack with a ranged weapon, this sequence is followed:

1. **DECLARE THE SHOT:** Pick a ranged weapon carried by the fighter, and pick an eligible enemy.
2. **CHECK THE RANGE:** Measure the range from the attacker to the target. If the target is outside the weapon's Long range, the attack automatically misses. The Firepower dice must still be rolled.
3. **MAKE THE HIT ROLL:** Make a BS check for the attacker, applying modifiers as listed below.
4. **TARGET IS PINNED:** When an Active fighter is hit by a ranged attack, they are automatically Pinned.
5. **RESOLVE HITS:** (See page 70 of the *Necromunda Rulebook*).

SHOOTING MODIFIERS:

- In partial cover (-1)
- In full cover (-2)
- Accuracy modifier (+/-?)
- Target is Engaged (-1)
- Target is Prone (-1, Long range only)

STRAY SHOTS: If an attack with a ranged weapon misses, there is a chance that other fighters, friendly or enemy, that are Engaging the target, or that are within 1" of the line along which the range between the attacker and the target was measured, will be hit.

If the attack misses, roll a D6 for each fighter that is at risk of being hit, starting with the fighter closest to the attacker. On a 1, 2 or 3, the fighter is hit by the attack. On a 4, 5 or 6, the shot misses them – move on to the next fighter at risk of being hit. If the attack would have caused more than one hit, follow this sequence for every hit.

CLOSE COMBAT SEQUENCE

When any fighter makes an attack with a close combat weapon whilst Engaging an enemy, this sequence is followed:

1. **TURN TO FACE:** The attacking fighter may turn to face any direction. Doing so reduces the result of any hit roll by 1.

2. **PICK WEAPONS:** The controlling player declares which weapons the fighter will use. A fighter can use up to two weapons with the Melee or Sidearm trait, but only one if it also has the Unwieldy trait. Alternatively, the fighter may make unarmed attacks.

3. **DETERMINE ATTACK DICE:** The number of Attack dice rolled is equal to the fighter's Attacks characteristic, plus the following modifiers:
   - Dual Weapons (+1)
   - Charging (+1)
   If the fighter is attacking with more than one weapon, the Attack dice must be split as evenly as possible. However, a fighter may only make one attack with a weapon with the Sidearm trait.

4. **DECLARE TARGETS:** Declare a target enemy fighter that is A) Engaged with the attacker and B) within their vision arc. Attacks can be split between eligible enemy fighters as the player wishes.

5. **MAKE HIT ROLL(S):** Make a WS check for the attacking fighter with each Attack dice. Roll separately for different weapons and/or different targets. Hit rolls may be modified by +1 for an assist from a friendly fighter also Engaged with the target, or by -1 for an enemy fighter also Engaging the attacker.

6. **RESOLVE HITS:** (As follows)

7. **REACTION ATTACKS:** If there are still enemies Engaged with the attacker, they may make Reaction attacks, following steps 1-6.

8. **CONSOLIDATE:** If all enemy fighters the attacker was Engaged with are now Prone and Seriously Injured or have gone Out of Action, they may move up to 2" in any direction.

RESOLVE HITS

When a fighter is hit by an attack, regardless of how it was inflicted, follow this sequence:

1. MAKE WOUND ROLL: Cross reference the weapon's Strength with the target's Toughness and roll on the table below:

Strength vs Toughness	D6 Roll Required
Is the Strength TWICE the Toughness or greater?	2+
Is the Strength GREATER than the Toughness?	3+
Is the Strength EQUAL to the Toughness?	4+
Is the Strength LOWER than the Toughness?	5+
Is the Strength HALF the Toughness or lower?	6+

2. OPPONENT MAKES A SAVE ROLL: If the attack causes a wound or leads to an Injury roll being made against the target the target, may be able to make an armour save.

Armour saves are made either:

- After the Wound roll is made but before the Wound is removed from the fighter, in which case the Wound is saved and not removed.
- If the attack has a Damage '-' characteristic and causes an Injury dice to be rolled against the fighter for any reason, a save roll is made before any Injury dice are rolled.

3. INFLICT DAMAGE: The target's Wounds characteristic is reduced by the weapon's Damage characteristic. If this reduces the target's Wounds to 0, roll Injury dice as described on page 71 of the *Necromunda Rulebook*.

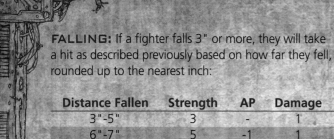

FALLING: If a fighter falls 3" or more, they will take a hit as described previously based on how far they fell, rounded up to the nearest inch:

Distance Fallen	Strength	AP	Damage
3"-5"	3	-	1
6"-7"	5	-1	1
8"-9"	7	-2	2
10"+	9	-3	3

A falling fighter is immediately Pinned and their activation ends. If they land on top of another fighter, they are also Pinned and suffer a hit identical to that taken by the falling fighter. Move the falling fighter the shortest possible distance so that the two are not overlapping.

If a falling fighter lands within ½" of a platform edge, they must pass an Initiative check or will fall again.

INJURY DICE AND LASTING INJURIES:

Each point of Damage removes one Wound. When a fighter is reduced to 0 Wounds, roll one Injury dice. If the weapon has additional points of Damage to cause after the last Wound has been removed, roll an additional Injury dice for each.

For example, if a fighter with two Wounds is hit by a weapon that causes three points of Damage, two Injury dice will be rolled. The first point of Damage removes a Wound, the second reduces the fighter to 0 Wounds and one Injury dice is rolled, and the third and final point of Damage will cause another Injury dice to be rolled.

Apply all of the results:

- **OUT OF ACTION:** The fighter is immediately removed from play.
- **SERIOUS INJURY:** The fighter is placed Prone and laid face-down. They may successfully recover in a later End phase. If Engaged, they may be vulnerable to a Coup de Grace (see Actions).
- **FLESH WOUND:** The fighter suffers a Flesh Wound, reducing their Toughness characteristic by 1. If a fighter is reduced to T0, they go Out of Action.

LASTING INJURIES:

If a fighter goes Out of Action during a Campaign game, immediately roll on the table below and apply the result:

D66	Lasting Injury
11	Lesson Learned. Into Recovery, +D3 Experience.
12-26	Out Cold. No effect.
31-45	Grievous Injury. Into Recovery.
46	Humiliated. Into Recovery, -1 Ld and Cl.
51	Head Injury. Into Recover, -1 Int and Wil.
52	Eye Injury. Into Recovery, -1 BS.
53	Hand Injury. Into Recovery, -1 WS.
54	Hobbled. Into Recovery, -1 M.
55	Spinal Injury. Into Recovery, -1 S.
56	Enfeebled. Into Recovery, -1 T.
61-65	Critical Injury. Dead, unless saved by a Doc.
66	Memorable Death. Dead – attacker gains +1 Experience.

NERVE TESTS

Each Active fighter must take a Nerve test when a friendly fighter is Seriously Injured or taken Out of Action within 3" of them. Engaged and Prone (Pinned or Seriously Injured) fighters do not need to test.

To make a Nerve test, make a Cool check for the fighter, adding 1 to the result for each Active friendly fighter within 3". If the check is passed, nothing happens. If the check is failed, the fighter becomes Broken and will immediately make a Running for Cover (Double) action. It the fighter is Standing and Active they move 2D6", if they are Prone and Pinned or Seriously Injured, they move half of their Movement characteristic. When a Broken fighter moves, they must attempt to end their move, in order of priority:

- So that they are more than 3" away from enemy fighters.
- So that they are out of line of sight of enemy fighters.
- In partial or full cover.
- As far away from any enemy fighters as possible.

If a Broken fighter is Standing and Engaged when activated, they must make an Initiative check. If it is passed, they must move as described above. Each enemy fighter that is Engaged with them makes an Initiative check, and if this is passed can make Reaction attacks before the Broken fighter is moved. If the Broken fighter fails the Initiative check, they remain Engaged and can perform no further actions.

EPHEMIS GLOOM-STALKER
UNDERWORLD SPECTERS
HOUSE DELAQUE

BRETHREN OF BONES
HOUSE CAWDOR

'BLESSED' BALDRYK

HAUBERK

COIF COFFINAIL

TIPPET

CYCLAS THE RATFINDER

COTTUS

THE SILENT ONES
HOUSE DELAQUE

Mandoth 'Dark Hand'

Cxauth 'The Night Serpent'

Iagorth

Naath 'Whisperblade'

Naegrath

Yartep

THE CARRION QUEENS
HOUSE ESCHER

RHOSINN

JELENA

REINA

TUMALA

ZARANN

MARIKA

THE IRONLORDS
HOUSE GOLIATH

Nox the Ripper

Skullshank

Varik

Drago

'Splitter' Korg

Grendel

THE SUMP DOGS
HOUSE ORLOCK

'Gunner' Ski

Lander

Mo Two-Fist

Zed 'Hackjaw'

Grimm

Roky

THE NEXUS NINES
HOUSE VAN SAAR

Lucien 'The Hammer'
Hargen

Hanselt

Lisbet 'Darkfinder'

Rutgeer

Koen

Larz
'Lightning Hand'

HIRED GUNS

Kria the Huntress

Gor Half-horn

Eyros Slagmyst

Grendl Grendlsen

Slate Merdena & Macula

Belladonna